The
TRIUMPHANT
PATIENT

The TRIUMPHANT PATIENT

GREG ANDERSON

THOMAS NELSON PUBLISHERS
NASHVILLE

Published in Nashville, Tennessee, by Thomas Nelson, Inc., and distributed in Canada by Lawson Falle, Ltd., Cambridge, Ontario.

The characters in this book are composites of real people but they are not intended to portray specific individuals.

Library of Congress Cataloging-in-Publication Data

Anderson, Greg, 1947–
    The triumphant patient / Greg Anderson.
        p.   cm.
ISBN 0-8407-7714-0
    1. Spiritual healing.   2. Patients—Conduct of life.   3. Patients—
Religious life.   I. Title.
BT732.5.A53   1992
362.1'9—dc20   92-4976
                                                                    CIP

Printed in the United States of America

1 2 3 4 5 6 7 — 97 96 95 94 93 92

TO
MY WIFE
LINDA
AND
OUR DAUGHTER
ERICA

Thank you for
your constant
love and support.

You, too, are
TRIUMPHANT!

ACKNOWLEDGMENTS

My deepest gratitude to God for his gift to me—the gift of life—and for the unlimited blessings I receive in serving.

Thank you to all who so generously gave of their time, creativity, and love in making this dream a reality.

A special thank you to all the friends of the Cancer Conquerors Foundation. I am so grateful for your acceptance and support. I treasure you.

A very special thank you to the Thomas Nelson Communications family—Ron Haynes for seeing the vision, Jane Jones for extraordinary editing, Bob Zaloba, Sara Fortenberry, and Pamela Clements for bringing the message to the world. I appreciate your professionalism, patience, and understanding.

Jane Jordan Browne, thank you for your enthusiasm. Governor and Mrs. George Leader, please accept my sincere gratitude for your constant encouragement and support. Carl Simonton, I am forever thankful that you pointed out the path. And Abigail "Dear Abby" Van Buren, my heartfelt appreciation for lifting my work from obscurity.

To all who seek to be triumphant and to the world, my love.

CONTENTS

INTRODUCTION

It was 1978 when my wife Bobbie and I started a group called Exceptional Cancer Patients (ECaP) to help people mobilize their full resources against their diseases. We sent out a hundred letters to patients. The letter suggested we could help them live better and longer through the techniques ECaP would teach them.

We expected hundreds of replies. We thought everyone who got a letter would tell several other cancer patients and bring them to the meeting. I began to get nervous about how to handle the crowd that would appear.

Twelve people showed up.

That was when I started to learn, firsthand, what patients are really like. I found there are three kinds.

In the middle of the spectrum of patients is the majority, about 60 to 70 percent. They are like actors auditioning for a part. They perform to satisfy their physicians. They act the way they think the doctors want them to act, hoping that then the doctors will do all the work and the medicine won't taste too bad.

About 15 to 20 percent of all patients unconsciously, or even consciously, wish to die. On some level they welcome cancer or another serious illness as a way to escape their problems.

At the other extreme are the 15 to 20 percent who are exceptional. The exceptional patients are not auditioning; they're being themselves. They refuse to play the victim. They educate themselves and become specialists in their own care. They question their doctors because they want to understand their treatment and participate in it. They demand dignity, personhood, and control, no matter what the course of their diseases. And they grow from their experiences.

This book, *The Triumphant Patient*, is a tribute to that spirit. It inspires. It instructs. It gives hope. In that sense, it heals. This book is required reading for anyone interested in health enhancement and life enrichment. It can help you triumph over the adversities and afflictions we are all subject to.

Triumphant doesn't mean living forever, but it does mean living now.

Enjoy!

Bernie S. Siegel, M.D.

WHAT THIS BOOK CAN DO FOR YOU

This book is written to suggest that you have profound choices in life no matter what your circumstances. Love, peace, serenity, wellness on the highest level can be yours.

I do not doubt this. I have watched these choices transform hundreds of people. I have had the experience myself. Some will say these assertions lack scientific proof. And others will suggest they may work for some but cannot be implemented in their own lives. But I disagree.

In 1984 I was given thirty days to live. Lung cancer had metastasized through my lymph system. My doctor told me there was nothing more medical science could do. He suggested it would be wise to get my affairs in order to prepare for my death.

It was a frightening time. My initial reaction was uncontrolled fear that quickly became self-pity. I became sicker, weaker, filled with despair. The lowest point was those days when I lost all hope.

Entirely too many people are defeated by loss of hope. Just as I did they say, "There is nothing I can do." Despair, resignation, and passivity set in. It doesn't have to be that way. There is always room for much hope in life.

On the physical level, there is a limit to how much we can do to create our own wellness. Genetics, environment, even life's bad breaks can add up to a difficult situation. But on the emotional and spiritual level, there is a triumphant outlook that can control, even co-create, our experiences of life. This level is without limits. And it is under our control, a matter of personal choice.

The concepts presented here are meant to be used in conjunction with the guidance and care of competent medical professionals. At no time do I suggest that these principles take the place of conventional medical care. Do not embark upon self-treatment of a serious illness without professional help.

There are a growing number of doctors who will form true partnerships with their patients. Find one. And use these ideas as part of a comprehensive wellness program.

Read this book with thought and care, and always with the question in mind, "How can I apply this in my life?" You will find this slim volume does not impose solutions. But it does suggest a radically different response to life. I hope you will allow its message to penetrate your thinking.

While the "how-to's" are included, I am hoping you will see much more than a group of techniques here. I want you to move a bit closer to understanding the truth about your ability to help in your healing on many levels. And I hope you will find the inspiration we all need when we make the commitment to walk the triumphant path.

I've used a parable format because it allows intimate and compassionate communication, something I find missing in clinical discussions of this subject. And I've devised the characters from composites of real people who have shared their experiences and feelings with me. Hopefully you will find in these characters the emotions you feel and will also find hope. If you are anything like me, you approach this subject with passion. I've simply tried to share those thoughts and *emotions* with you. Know that you are not alone when you experience them. But also realize you can get those thoughts and emotions working for you, not against you.

This format communicates truth with strength, clarity, honesty, and simplicity. I believe the result is a book that can be read profitably without being painstakingly studied.

Most of all keep your hope alive. What you believe about your ability to respond to life's circumstances, how you handle emotional conflicts, plus your personal decision to walk in the Light, all work together to make a huge difference in your experience of illness or disability, and of life.

Welcome to the world of the triumphant!

Greg Anderson
Fullerton, California

April 1992

Chapter 1

THE SEARCH
FOR SOLUTIONS

T he woman was devastated.

Her doctor had just told her she had a life-threatening illness. He used the word *terminal* and said there was nothing more he could do.

"You have perhaps a year," he said. "I can't say for sure. I'm sorry. We'll do our best to make you comfortable."

She was in shock. It was a death sentence. She was going to *die!*

And there was nothing she could do, nothing anyone could do.

At times she was numb. She just sat in a chair, not moving or speaking. She couldn't eat. She was exhausted, but she couldn't sleep for more than a few minutes at a time.

The future was so bleak.

"Everything is okay," she told herself. "There must

have been a mistake. That's it! The tests were wrong. They were somebody else's tests! It's not me. No! It's not me!"

But the doctor said the tests weren't wrong. He said no one had made a mistake. She couldn't believe him. She just couldn't believe it was true.

"Okay," she said, "maybe the tests weren't wrong, but the prognosis is. The problem really isn't what they said it is! Or, even if it is, it's not as serious as they think. Yes, that's right. It's not serious. It will soon go away."

She did try to keep her spirits up, but it was so hard. A constant mental chatter badgered her every minute, and she couldn't turn it off.

What about her family? Will her husband be okay? What will happen to the children? What about the house? Who will take care of things? "Will they miss me? Oh, God! They'll forget me!"

The worst part was the fear. How does it feel to die? Does it hurt? Will it hurt more than she can stand? If it gets really bad, will everyone leave her to die alone?

She was a prisoner—a prisoner of fear and illness and death, a prisoner of all the thoughts in her mind. Panic was her constant companion. She was over-whelmed by it.

And she couldn't control the weeping. Without warning the tears would begin, and they didn't stop until she was completely spent. No one understood. No one could understand, not even those who loved her. One minute she wanted to die, to just get it over with. The next she wanted to live, for her life to return to normal.

She was isolated, cut off from life and hope. No one

had ever experienced such desolation and despair. There was no hope. And soon there would be no life.

She withdrew from her family, thinking that would make her death easier for them. But her family resisted. They said they wanted to help her. They said they loved her. They said they needed her. They said they wanted her to live.

Angrily she ordered them out. "Go away," she screamed. "Leave me alone. You're just trying to cheer me up!"

They left her alone, tiptoeing around, speaking softly to each other, trying not to upset her. And they looked at her with sadness in their eyes.

The depression was overpowering—spiraling, dark, all-consuming depression. She felt like she was already dead. Sometimes she hoped it would be over quickly.

One day she went for a walk, and she looked at the people she passed. They were laughing and having a good time with their families and friends. There was a woman, a grandmother, pushing a baby in a stroller. She was talking to the baby, her voice warm and loving and happy. The baby laughed and clapped her hands in response.

"I'll never see my grandchildren," the woman thought, and a great sadness came over her.

Then gradually the sadness became anger and the anger turned to rage. "This isn't fair! I deserve to see my grandchildren. I've been a good person—it's not fair for me to die.

"Look at all these people—they're well. And I'm dying. Why do they deserve better than I do? I want to live too."

Resentment burned inside her.

She'd been betrayed by life, and by God . . . if there really was a God. And these thoughts began to show in her every action and word.

Sometimes she was rude; sometimes she lashed out with anger; sometimes she wouldn't speak at all. She didn't like herself when she did these things, but she couldn't help herself.

It was all so difficult. Nothing mattered anymore.

"Is this all there is?" she wondered. "You're born; you live a while; and you die. And that's it?"

She'd always thought there would be more time. After the children were grown, she'd . . . When her husband got a promotion and they moved, she'd . . . When she had more time, she'd . . . But there wasn't going to be more time.

One day her friend Grace called. In a friendly way Grace chatted about many things and it was nice. For a few minutes the woman thought about something other than herself. But eventually Grace mentioned "the illness." That was the way the woman thought of it—"the illness," as if it had a life of its own and was somehow disconnected from her—and she always dreaded the time someone would mention it.

Usually people would say they were sorry and try to reassure her that a miracle would come along and make things right. She knew they were trying to help, but it didn't help. It only made her angry and then the hopelessness and depression would be worse than ever.

But this time was different. Grace didn't say those things that showed she didn't understand and that seemed so patronizing.

"I don't know how you feel," she said, "but I know someone who does. He's lived through circumstances that are very similar to yours. I think he might help you. Would you like to meet him?"

The woman hesitated. No, she resisted. In a way she didn't want to let anyone in. In a way she was comfortable with her isolation. She doubted that anyone had ever felt the way she did, and she was skeptical that anyone could truly understand how she felt. Most of all she believed that no one could help. As much as she wanted people to understand her pain and to help her, she no longer wanted to talk about it with anyone. But she didn't want simply to be brave and endure it. She wanted someone to take this problem away and make her well. She wanted to wake up and find it had all been a bad dream.

"Who is this person?" she asked.

"They call him the *Triumphant Patient*," Grace answered.

"The Triumphant Patient?" the woman laughed mockingly. "That's the most ridiculous name I've ever heard. What kind of person is this Triumphant Patient?"

"I know it sounds strange," Grace said. "But I assure you that he is quite real. He has learned some valuable principles about wellness that have helped him and others he has worked with to live life to the fullest. He has a whole network of other triumphant patients and they've all been through experiences like yours. I think it is something you might want to explore.

"Let me give you his number. Then, someday when you are feeling particularly down, you can give him a call. Take the number and keep it by your phone just in case."

"Well," said the woman. "I guess it wouldn't hurt."

As she wrote the number on a card, she thought about what Grace had said. She had said, "It's something you might want to explore," and that was different from anything anyone else had ever said to her. Her doctor said she *must* do this and that. Her family frequently tried to impose on her their ideas of how she should behave, even though they were gentle about it. Her other friends and acquaintances also had their own ideas of what she should do.

But Grace had said "explore." That meant she had a choice.

As she put the card on the wall by the phone, she was fairly certain she'd never call the Triumphant Patient. She was almost embarrassed by the idea. It seemed ridiculous to think for even a second that he could understand and help. Besides, she didn't want to get her hopes up just to be disappointed.

For several days she found herself thinking again about Grace's call. When she passed the phone, she'd notice that the card was there, waiting. A couple of times she read the number and even put her hand on the receiver. But she didn't pick it up. She was afraid. Yet she couldn't get her friend's words out of her mind, "It's something you might want to explore."

Finally, before she could change her mind, she dialed the number. She'd just see what he had to say. It certainly couldn't make things worse.

His voice was kind and gentle, and listening to him did make her feel more calm. When he suggested they get together to talk in person the next afternoon, she agreed.

In a small way, she was encouraged. She decided she would listen to him; she would try to be open. In fact, she realized she was looking forward to meeting the Triumphant Patient.

Chapter 2

BELIEVE IN THE POWER OF HOPE

The next afternoon, as she approached the home of the Triumphant Patient, the woman's mind was a muddle of conflicting emotions. She was embarrassed and she felt vulnerable.

"Why am I here?" she asked herself. "What could this man possibly know?" Her doctor had said there was no hope for her, so why subject herself to something that wouldn't help anyway?

She wanted to turn back and slip away. It would be easy to get in her car and simply go home. Yes, that would be easier. She would go home. And what would she do when she got there? Just get in bed and wait to die? Accept her fate in silence? Give in to the depression and despair?

Well, how long could it take to meet this man and hear what he had to say? An hour? She had precious little time left, but she could spare an hour, especially since there wasn't anything else to do. If she went home she'd only have to deal with the depression and the loneliness.

In the short conversation she'd had with this man, the one her friend had called the Triumphant Patient, she had sensed something different about him. Maybe he did know something that would help.

"Good afternoon," he said as he held open the door to his home. "Welcome. Please come in."

Immediately the woman sensed warmth. She was very comfortable with the pleasant manner, easy smile, and honesty of the man she had come to visit— the Triumphant Patient. She wasn't certain why, but she felt like an equal, and for the longest time she hadn't felt equal to anyone.

The man led her to a deck at the rear of the house where there was a lovely view and refreshments awaited them. He asked her to make herself comfortable. Then he began to talk with her, his manner friendly and unhurried.

Before long, he asked the woman to briefly describe her illness and the prognosis. But he didn't ask her to dwell on the details and technicalities of her illness. Instead he gently asked about her interpretation of her physical problems.

"Do you believe this prognosis?" he asked. "Do you feel the doctors' 'terminal' diagnosis is correct?" "How much confidence do you have in your medical team?" "Do you sense there is anything you can do to help yourself?"

He asked her questions, but not in a threatening way. He was compassionate. The way he asked the questions demonstrated that he understood and cared. His wisdom reassured her.

"Share with me your true feelings about your medical team," he said. He was skillful at bringing out someone's emotions. And he did it without effort or threat.

She was surprised to hear herself sharing her true feelings about her doctors and nurses and technicians. "They certainly have what seems to be the latest technology," she said, "but sometimes, when I leave there, I feel like I have just been through enemy territory."

"Tell me what you mean," he responded.

"I have to fight for every bit of information. It makes me so damned mad!" She was shocked at her own language. She seldom used those kinds of words. Suddenly she realized that she was very angry at her doctor.

"Whenever I go to that office, I have to wait. I understand that they probably have some unforeseen things interrupt their schedule. But always? Every time I go?

"No way! Don't they have any consideration for my time and my schedule? They don't seem to. And I hate it."

She was surprised at herself again. Her anger was intense. She realized she was leaning forward and gripping the arms of her chair. Her whole body was tense.

The Triumphant Patient sat quietly, observing her reactions.

"It's not just the waiting though, it's that they don't tell me anything and I can't fully understand what they are doing.

"For example, a couple of weeks ago I had a test. It was excruciating. I had to swallow an awful-tasting chalky solution and keep it down while they took X-rays. It was awful, and I threw up. But when I asked the technician why I needed this done, she simply said, 'The doctor ordered it.'

"It was terrible. And I felt so degraded and humiliated. They didn't seem to care that I was hurting or that I was frightened. Mostly I felt like an object—that I wasn't supposed to have feelings."

She wiped tears from her eyes.

"I believe I understand," he said. "It is difficult to have confidence in a medical team that lacks compassion. Yet a medical team in whom you have confidence is fundamental to getting well. May I share with you some of my experience?"

She nodded and leaned back, trying to relax and compose herself.

"I had to 'dismiss' a doctor from my team."

"You can do that?" she asked, incredulous.

"Of course you can. Doctors work for you; you don't work for them. You are the one in charge of your team members. And I didn't have confidence in all of my team.

"So I fired my surgeon. And I went about assembling a team I trusted. I had tests retaken. I got second opinions. At one point, I even had a third opinion."

"I can't do that," she said. "My insurance won't cover it."

"Neither did mine. So I paid for it out of my own pocket. I wasn't going to let the lack of insurance coverage stand in my way. I was ready to take charge!"

The woman couldn't help but notice the man's determination as he recalled his experience. This is a person who was strong when he needed to be strong, she thought. She felt great respect for him.

"And I didn't do it so much because of the technical diagnosis," he continued. "I did it to boost my confidence. It gave me peace of mind. I studied. I worked. In a real sense I became an expert on my illness. I even researched and suggested a new way to administer treatment."

She was surprised. "They let you make decisions?"

"I certainly contributed," he said with a smile. "After all, who had a vested interest? I did! It is a patient's duty to take charge.

"I insisted that all information be shared with me, and in a timely manner. I demanded explanations for each and every test. I wanted to understand all treatments. And I took personal responsibility for my wellness. This generated a great deal of hope in what was initially described to me as a hopeless situation."

"That might've been easy for you to do," said the woman. "But it's not the same with me. My situation is different."

"Tell me why," said the Triumphant Patient.

Tears came to her eyes, and panic and self-pity were evident on her face.

"I'm going to die. It's hopeless." And the tears came, the uncontrollable weeping she had been fighting for some time to avoid. The man brought some tissues to her and waited quietly until she was spent.

"I'm sorry I can't control my emotions," she whispered. "This happens so often. Forgive me for crying."

"Don't apologize for the tears," he soothed. "They are nothing to be embarrassed about. Tears are a natural way of releasing emotions. I think of them as God's method of cleansing the soul.

"But more important than the tears," he continued, "is your response to what your doctors told you. Few things are more sensitive and delicate than the psychological and emotional environment in which a patient is treated. In your case, you've been done a real disservice. What your doctor told you has caused you to despair."

Still wiping away her tears, the woman shook her head. "It's hopeless. A year! I can't believe it! I had so much to do. Is this all there is to life? There must be more."

And again she began to sob.

The Triumphant Patient realized that restoring the woman's hope was the first task. Without hope, there would be no triumphant outcome. Softly, quietly, gently, he began.

"As unfair to you as the doctor's words were, I want you to realize now that you have a choice in how to respond to them.

"Some people respond by stoically accepting the prognosis. When you ask these people how they're doing, they say, 'fine' and force a grin. But you know that inside they're not fine.

"Other people respond with fear and panic. Sometimes the situation creates emotional hysteria. Their worlds come crashing in around them. You may be feeling some of this."

She nodded.

"A third choice, the triumphant response, is proactive. Triumphant patients refuse to be victims. Instead, they take charge of their own care. They insist that they have full information so they can participate in their wellness programs. And they use health challenges as opportunities for personal growth.

"There are different levels of wellness that triumphant patients address. On the physical level there is conventional medical treatment. They form healing partnerships with their medical teams and take very active roles in their treatment.

"Beyond conventional medicine, triumphant patients take charge of their diet and exercise habits. They choose to stop committing suicide with their knives and forks and televisions and easy chairs. They choose to live life on the highest possible level, no matter what the prognosis.

"Medical treatment, diet, and exercise are the core elements of wellness on the physical level.

"But triumphant patients don't stop there," he continued. "They address the mental and emotional areas of their lives. They learn about and tap the power of their minds to contribute to their wellness.

"They develop a positive set of beliefs and attitudes, boost their self-images, and enhance their abilities to manage stress more effectively. They learn and use the principles of emotional wellness.

"And they strengthen their spiritual resources. They practice non-judgmental love, forgive themselves and others, and do their best to follow God's will as best they understand it. They constantly practice gratitude for living."

The Triumphant Patient paused and leaned a little forward. Again he smiled gently at the woman. He wanted to be certain he had her full attention. It was vital that she understand what he would say next.

"Responding with stoic acceptance is equivalent to absolute despair. Responding with panic is giving in to fear. But the third choice, the triumphant patient choice, is based in hope.

"If you want to help yourself, truly help yourself, I suggest you consider the possibilities in the third choice. I encourage you to choose hope."

The woman had stopped crying and was listening intently.

"But I have a physical problem," she said. "What you are suggesting is emotional, even spiritual. That doesn't relate to my illness."

"Oh, it does," he said. "And it is a documented scientific fact. Evidence now exists that depression, directly linked to despair, can actually compromise the effectiveness of a body's disease-fighting cells. In reality our emotions do affect us on the physical level. Hope is an emotional and spiritual choice, and hope—active, positive, living hope—can impact all areas of our lives, including our physical well-being.

"It's critical that you understand this one point: Your decision to choose hope will affect every part of your well-being. And you must also realize that fear and despair have negative influences on your well-being."

The woman was skeptical, and she questioned the entire premise.

"I can see how hope might help me emotionally or spiritually if I were inclined to believe any of that. But to help on a physical level? I think that's ridiculous."

"My friend," the Triumphant Patient said with a smile, "I realize these beliefs are not for everyone. But I ask you to give me just a moment to make the case.

"The well-known phrase, 'While there is life there is hope,' has far deeper meaning and power in reverse: *While there is hope there is life*. Hope comes first, and life follows.

"Hope gives power to life. Hope encourages life to continue, to grow, to reach out, to go on.

"Hope is like a candle in the depths of darkness. It changes our ability to see. With hope we perceive challenges where before there were only threats. Hope finds answers where there were only questions. And hope knows love where there was only fear.

"Hope is the miracle medicine of the soul. It is the power behind the will to live. It is a doctor's strongest ally. But a doctor cannot inject it, for hope can only be prescribed. It is the single indispensable ingredient of wellness.

"Many choices will face you in the days and weeks ahead. But none, not one, will be more important for you than choosing hope. I pray you will, for the greatest secret of wellness is to fill your mind and heart with hope."

The woman looked at this gentle, kind man who had spoken to her so earnestly. Was he kidding himself? Her doctor had shown her the test results. And he had drawn a sketch to explain the situation. Her problem was a molecular and biological reality. It was not a figment of her imagination. She was doubtful. How could hope or any other emotion change or in any way affect what was going on inside her body?

In fact, her doctor had warned her not to expect any benefit from the very thing this man was talking about. The doctor had said, "This is very serious. I don't want to give you any false hope."

Is that what the Triumphant Patient was trying to do? Was he planting seeds of false hope? Was this just a cruel hoax? Suddenly she was angry.

"I think you're misguided," she said quite sharply. "My doctor, a specialist who has seen hundreds of cases like mine, explained the situation clearly to me. And he warned about false hope. The reality is that I have a physical illness. And I think your premise creates a sense of false hope that will only lead to disappointment."

The Triumphant Patient had heard this argument before many times. And as always, it made him uncomfortable. He didn't consider it a personal attack, but it concerned him because many people were so focused on the down side of their physical problems they refused to even consider other outcomes.

"Listen carefully," he said. "Hope is a medical reality. If your doctor is going to do all that is within his power to help you, he must not compromise his efforts by creating a psychological and emotional environment of defeat and fatalism. But your doctor has done this, and it does not serve you well."

The woman was quiet. What the Triumphant Patient said was true. Her doctor had created a very negative environment for her. He had taken all hope from her.

"Telling some patients the worst possible outcome can often help to bring about that outcome. But tell me this," continued the Triumphant Patient, "did your doctor balance his negative prognosis by telling you the best possible outcome?"

The woman shook her head. "I think he told me the only possible outcome," she whispered.

"The point I'm making is this: People tend to move

along the path of their expectations. Your expectations are anything but positive. The wise physician will balance his concern over a patient's chances with encouraging the patient's will to live.

"And that is where hope makes a critical difference. Assuming a stance of positive expectation, even in the face of serious medical circumstances, is not false hope. In fact, in my opinion, false hope does not exist. There is only hope—reasonable hope.

"I can't guarantee you recovery. But I can guarantee you a better life, no matter how long you live, if you will embrace hope.

"When you raise the issue of false hope, it suggests that people should never be hopeful if there is a good chance they might meet with disappointment. That represents a dim view that does not align with reality."

The woman was defensive, "Well, I am just being realistic. I want to know my situation as it really is."

The Triumphant Patient carefully considered his next words.

"A life view that does not include hope simply is not a realistic life view," he said. "It is a pessimistic life view.

"Understand this clearly. By holding such beliefs, you may avoid disappointment. But these expectations will probably actively shape negative outcomes."

That sounds like truth, thought the woman. She had been emotionally crippled since she learned her prognosis. And the devastation was at times overwhelming. What the Triumphant Patient said about guaranteeing a better life—no matter how long the life might be—made sense.

Her parents had always prided themselves as being realists, and their view of life was often very dim. She could remember how it bothered her at times. Maybe she had learned from her parents to view her own life the way they felt about theirs.

She realized clearly that she would have to make a decision. Would she believe the best or the worst? Would she act on her fears or her hopes? It was apparent that she had a significant choice before her.

She looked at the Triumphant Patient. He had been studying her quietly, searching for clues to what she was thinking, attempting to gauge her reactions.

"You have a series of choices ahead of you," he said. "Let's take a moment to understand where you really are on this journey and what you might have to do.

"First, you said you have reservations about your medical team. Is that right?"

"Yes, I do," she responded.

"Have you sought out a second opinion?"

"No, I haven't," she said.

"Get one immediately. And this in no way questions the abilities of your current medical team."

"I've thought about getting a second opinion, but I was afraid it would make my doctor angry."

"It shouldn't," said the Triumphant Patient shaking his head in disgust. He had heard this response before. Many people are frightened of their doctors.

"The best doctors will not perceive a second opinion as a threat, either personally or financially. And if they do react negatively, that is another signal to consider in evaluating whether you want to retain them.

"In your case, the first step in breaking out of this stance of despair and being able to choose hope might be linked to getting a second opinion. I want you to consider this as decision number one."

The woman thought about the Triumphant Patient's

advice. And she made a mental note to act on this suggestion. She shook her head to let him know she
would carefully consider what he said.

"Good," he said. "Then, ask yourself, 'How is my
attitude?' 'Can I adopt a more positive attitude toward
this illness?' 'Might I choose one of hope?'"

"I don't see any room for a positive attitude," the
woman retorted. "There's just no hope."

"If you choose to explore the triumphant patient
path, you will see there is the possibility for hope in all
situations. This belief will mean drastic change for
you.

"What about diet? Are you giving your body the
best in fuel?"

"Well, probably not," she responded. "At least not
right now. I just don't have much appetite."

"Diet and nutrition choices are another part of the
triumphant journey. All these elements work together
for greater wellness.

"The same is true of exercise, of a balance between
your work and play, of your relationships, even of the
spiritual choices you make. Each has a part to play in
getting well. And together I believe they may even
help cure."

The woman listened intently, wondering how the
Triumphant Patient could speak with such authority.
What were his qualifications?

"Tell me your story," she said. "How did you come
to have these beliefs?"

"It was lung cancer," he said. "The doctor put his
hand on my shoulder and said that surgery was the
only answer. The lung would have to come out.

"They performed surgery, but four months later a

growth began protruding from my neck. Again surgery. It was malignant. The cancer had spread. They could not remove it. The surgeon closed the incision and told me to get my affairs in order. According to statistics, I had a life expectancy of thirty days."

The woman was astonished. "My prognosis is better than that. How did you do it?"

The Triumphant Patient stopped. He looked intently at the woman, wanting to make a forceful statement that would break through her doubts and resistance.

"After my second surgery, I was very frightened. I believed the doctor's prognosis and lost all hope. The fear of my life suddenly ending paralyzed me.

"I was sitting on the couch watching my daughter play with a doll when suddenly I thought, 'I will not live to see her grow up.' It was the lowest point for me. I don't know of any deeper despair. Tears filled my eyes. I was mired in self-pity. I thought my life was over.

"The next words I spoke were full of anger and fear. I cried out, 'Oh, God, what can I do?'

"Somehow, through the tears, the anger, and the fear, a different thought came to me. It was as if someone were saying, 'You may not be given long to live, but live as long as you are given.'

"Hope was in that thought. It was a seed that I knew needed special care and attention. It provided tremendous encouragement for me during the countless down times that followed. I knew that every day I had to rededicate myself to living that one day for all it was worth. I knew I needed to live my life filled with hope, no matter how long I might live.

"Looking at my daughter, I thought, 'I may not be

here to love her tomorrow. But I am here today. I'll show her my love *now*.'

"That is the heart of becoming a triumphant patient."

Again the woman was skeptical, even scornful.

"That sounds so simplistic," she said, "so ethereal. There certainly must be more."

"Yes, there is more. Much more," he said. "But living for today, doing the best I could here and now to make love my aim, changed not only my health, but my entire life. And it can do the same for you.

"No one is going to force you to walk the triumphant path. You must choose. And don't take my word for it. Talk to others. In fact, if you want to take this journey, your first assignment is to visit several people, one each week. You will learn the major principles of becoming triumphant.

"If you complete the assignment, come back and we will talk about why the triumphant path works, and we'll look at the real benefits of becoming a triumphant patient. Is this something that you might like to do?"

It seemed so simple, as if there were some sort of formula to implement and then everything would be okay. But she was reluctant and unsure of all that the Triumphant Patient had told her. Still she heard herself saying, "Okay, what do I have to lose?"

The Triumphant Patient looked intently at her. "All you have to lose," he said, "is hopelessness. I'll set up the first appointment for you. It will be with Maria.

"Before you go to see her, give careful thought to choosing wellness in body, mind, and spirit. And choose hope! While you have hope, you have life!"

As the woman drove home she thought about her visit with the Triumphant Patient, and she smiled when she remembered how afraid she'd been to meet him.

"What did I think he would say to me?" she asked herself. "Suggest that I abandon all medical treatments? Or try some unconventional program?"

She'd had no idea that he had been in a situation that was more serious than hers. In fact, she'd hardly allowed herself to consider that anyone might have ever suffered with illness the way she was suffering. For the first time since her doctor had told her she was gravely ill, she realized that others had faced the same kind of life challenge and that they too had been afraid and angry, even filled with despair.

She felt comforted. She had found someone who understood how she felt. He had not faulted her for her tears. He had not told her to smile through her pain and die with dignity. He had not recounted all her blessings and told her to be thankful.

He had said, "Take charge of your wellness and choose hope. While there's hope, there is life."

She did not know what lay ahead, but she had a different perspective. She was still afraid and she was still angry, but the Triumphant Patient had planted a small seed in her mind—a seed of hope.

Chapter 3

Belief Becomes Biology

"I believed no one cared . . . that my life no longer had meaning . . . and I questioned if there was any reason to continue living."

Maria's voice was calm and quiet as she recounted her experience.

"Inside I was screaming, 'I want out!' 'I don't want to suffer anymore!' 'I can't take it anymore!' 'It's all too much!'

"And that's when I found myself on the beach in the middle of the night with a debilitating disease in my body and a revolver in my hand."

Maria paused and closed her eyes. Retelling her story caused all the emotion to wash over her again.

In the silence that followed, the woman sat stunned. The story Maria told her had happened over twenty years before, but the woman could feel the pain and despair as if it were happening to her right then.

Maria's five-year-old daughter was ill, and during the following year, the child grew worse. One cold winter day, just before the holidays, the little girl died.

Maria was inconsolable, and she went into a deep depression. Over the next year, her life got worse. Her husband developed a drug and alcohol dependency. He left her, and they filed for divorce.

She lost her job and was forced to live with her parents. But beyond sharing their home with Maria, they were unable to help her. They were frail and needed her to care for them. At a time when she needed to heal, she was also burdened with caring for others.

She began to experience excruciating physical pain throughout her body and the jerking of involuntary muscle tremors. Within a few months she was diagnosed with multiple sclerosis.

Then one night, when it was all too much, she ran out of hope.

Maria opened her eyes and looked steadily at the woman.

"I believed the world would be a better place if I were no longer part of it," she whispered. "I thought I could solve my personal suffering by ending my life. It seemed to be the only answer."

"What stopped you from using the gun?" asked the woman.

"As I stood there on the beach reviewing all my troubles," Maria said, "I remembered a gift someone had given me when I was in the hospital for tests. It was a small, gold medallion on a chain. Although at the time it was given to me it didn't mean much, on the beach I remembered the medallion had a verse on it.

"I can only guess why that thought came to my mind at that moment, but something told me to search for the necklace.

"I vaguely remembered seeing it a couple of weeks before at the bottom of my purse, and I dug frantically, searching for it. Finally I dumped everything in my purse right on the sand. And then I found it."

Maria touched the necklace she was wearing. "Here it is," she said, as she removed it and handed it to the woman. "I'd like you to read it."

"The Triumphant Patient's Creed," the woman read aloud.

> *Hope reigns in my life today.*
> *My illness does not rule me.*
> *Daily I seek to*
> *Acknowledge the physical,*
> *Be positive in the mental,*
> *Transcend the emotional,*
> *And anchor in the spiritual,*
> *Knowing that God's peace is my goal.*
> *Thank you, Lord, for today's blessings!*

"That verse changed my life," Maria said. "In fact, it *saved* my life. And I have worn the necklace ever since."

The woman looked again at the medallion and then at Maria. "Do you think this has magical powers?" she asked.

"No," Maria said with a smile. "The power is not in the medallion. It's in what the message taps in me.

You see, the triumphant patient's journey is all right there. Look at it.

"The Creed begins with hope. You've already talked with the Triumphant Patient about choosing hope, and you've heard of its importance. You are beginning to understand that if hope reigns, the illness, the troubles, cannot rule you.

"The night I went to the beach with a pistol in my hand, I had turned the leadership of my life over to my problems. I was allowing my troubles to be my guiding force. It was one thing after another. Death of a child. Divorce. Caregiving. Illness. Loss. Grief. Jealousy. Resentment. Powerlessness. Pain. Isolation. Exhaustion. All of it led to despair.

"At the water's edge, in the middle of the night, it became very clear what I'd done. I'd chosen to be passive and fatalistic, to view myself as a helpless victim.

"Then I found that necklace. It said 'Hope reigns in my life. My illness does not rule me.' And I wondered, 'Might it be possible for me to be hopeful?'"

The woman was listening intently, absorbed by the drama of Maria's journey.

"There is a part of me, and there is a part of you, that at will can choose how to react to the circumstances of life," Maria continued. "Our choices are to respond either with hope or with despair.

"I decided to give hope a chance, to tap that part of me that operates on a higher plane, the part we all have that calls us to a higher level of response. When we do that, we honor the great person within us. This is our best spirit, and it flows from a source that I too often had overlooked."

"It sounds like you're going to tell me to turn to God," the woman snapped, feeling defensive.

"No, I'm only telling you my own experience," Maria replied calmly. "You can draw your own conclusions.

"The Triumphant Patient is very careful not to impose any beliefs on others. But at the same time, he is quite open in discussing his own journey. I try to share my experience that way too. But no one is going to force you to do or believe anything against your will. I can assure you of that."

The woman understood, and she remembered her promise to herself to be open. But it was difficult at times.

Maria tried again to gauge the woman. She realized that one must be so careful in what is said to some people, and how it is presented. Just wanting to be helpful isn't enough. Skill is needed also. And each person is a unique experience. Perhaps it would help to bring the woman back to the Creed.

"Take a look at the necklace again," Maria said. "What the Creed reminds us to do is to give leadership of our lives to the power of hope. And the next sentence gives us the plan for doing it. See the first line? 'Daily I seek . . .' What a powerful reminder!

"Becoming triumphant was not a onetime overnight exercise for me. I didn't suddenly leave the water's edge with all my troubles gone. My daughter was still dead. I was still divorced from an alcoholic. I was still unemployed. My parents were still elderly and frail and in need of daily care. I still had multiple sclerosis."

"I can't imagine how you felt that night," said the woman, "but if I put myself in your place, I feel cer-

tain I would want to put an end to all of it. I think I'd
have used the gun. So how can you say that some
words written on a little trinket made a difference?

"Once you'd read the words, what was different?"

"I was different," Maria said.

"How?" the woman asked.

"When I picked the medallion out of the sand and
read the Creed, all the circumstances of my life were
still the same, but *I* was transformed—in my mind. I
decided I would no longer be a passive victim. I decided to acknowledge my daughter's death and grieve
for her. I decided to acknowledge that my marriage
had ended and grieve that loss. I decided to acknowledge that the man I loved and married had been unable to give the power of hope to his own life and to
stop resenting him for that. I decided to acknowledge
that my parents needed care and to love them and care
for them in whatever way I could. I decided to acknowledge my illness and to begin that day learning
about it and how I could help myself. I decided that for
just one day I would live, for that one day I would put
control of my life in the power of hope.

"And the next day I would do it again.

"I've lived that way ever since. It has been a daily,
step-by-step journey, and *daily* is the key word. Each
day I vow to live this day to the fullest, no matter what
the circumstances, no matter what the conditions.

"Concentrating on today, not yesterday or tomorrow, and making the best of this moment makes me
triumphant. In spite of my problems and no matter
what the outcome, I have lived with joy, *today!* That is
wellness!

"So often we rob ourselves of today. We become

mired in the if-onlys of the past and the what-ifs of the future. We lament 'If only I hadn't . . .' 'If only I weren't . . .' 'If only I hadn't been . . .' But we can't live this moment fully if we are spending time trying to overcome what we did or didn't do in the past.

"We rob ourselves of the moment also when we spend our energies on worrying about the future. 'What if I get sick?' 'What if the doctor is right?' 'What if . . .' and the list goes on and on. We miss today by being consumed with fear of the future.

"Both ways of thinking are destructive. Our only hope for wellness comes in *this* moment. This means ceasing the if-onlys of the past and the what-ifs of the future and deciding to make the best of right now.

"We can live our lives, despite all our troubles, in a celebration of the blessings of this moment. And we make the future an extension of these moments of wellness. This produces triumphant results no matter what the outcome."

The woman couldn't help admiring Maria. She had such a powerful story. She wasn't sure of all Maria had to say, but the woman did respect her. In a real sense, Maria was a heroine, and she was triumphant! But still, the woman had questions. It is one thing to have hope, but isn't that an issue of the mind? She was dealing with issues of a physical nature.

"Isn't living for today just a form of denial?" she asked.

"Not at all," Maria replied, thinking that the woman was bright and insightful. If she would just open her mind and be more receptive, she certainly could become triumphant. Maria prayed silently that she could reach the woman.

"The Creed addresses denial with the next line," Maria said. "It says, 'Acknowledge the physical.' I like that. I like the word *acknowledge*. We are not denying the illness, and we are not fooling ourselves into thinking we have no problems. But neither are we allowing those problems to overwhelm us. We acknowledge them. Acknowledgment is not denial. Do you see that?"

"Yes," the woman responded, "Yes, I understand!

"Denial is going about saying, 'This can't be happening to me!' 'Oh, no, not me!' Denial is saying, 'Everything will be all right—it will all go away.' Denial is saying, 'I really don't have a problem. I'll ignore it.'"

Maria was pleased, enthused that her new friend was learning so quickly.

"That's what I've been doing," the woman continued. "I've been raging, trying to find some one or some thing to blame. I've been allowing despair to overwhelm me, just as you did, and that took you to the beach ready to end your life.

"But at the beach, you acknowledged your circumstances. I can do that. I can acknowledge my circumstances. And right now I will."

The woman straightened her body, preparing to make an important statement.

"I acknowledge that I have a serious illness. It is an illness that my doctor has said is terminal."

The woman paused. She looked intently at Maria, and said, "It's still the same, isn't it? How did that help me?"

Maria was quiet for a moment. She realized that the tiny seed of hope planted by the Triumphant Patient had taken root in the woman's mind.

"Oh, my new friend, it helped you a great deal, much more than you know right now," Maria said. "In acknowledging your illness, you took from it its power to control all of your life. Now that you have acknowledged your illness, you can move to triumph over it."

Again Maria was quiet, giving the woman time to think, giving the seed of hope time to grow.

"I cannot tell you how much I want to be triumphant," the woman said. "But I'm afraid. Deep within me there is fear—fear that this won't work, fear that in spite of everything I will die, fear that if I believe you I'll wake up one morning and realize I was fooled."

"You've just done two things," Maria said, "and they were both significant steps for you to take—beginning steps on the triumphant journey.

"You've acknowledged your illness and you've acknowledged your fear. I sense that this is the first time you've actually acknowledged either of them."

"Yes," the woman whispered. "You're right. I've been yelling and screaming and weeping. But right now is the first time that I have really acknowledged that I am greatly afraid."

Maria smiled and reached for the woman's hand.

"Excellent," she said. "You have great courage, my friend. You've acknowledged both your illness and your fear. Now you're ready to move on, for once you understand and accept your illness and your fears, they no longer have power over you. You're now free to do the work of wellness.

"Please look at the Creed again. You have acknowledged your physical illness and the next three thoughts will help you become triumphant. They are: *Be positive in the mental; Transcend the emotional;* and *Anchor in the spiritual.*

"Believing in yourself and in your own self-healing capabilities is being mentally positive. Those who are facing illness can help themselves by changing their minds, by deciding to be positive rather than negative.

"Next, we can transcend! Isn't that an inspiring thought? We can choose to rise above our negative feelings and embrace the higher levels of love and joy. We can decide to let the great person within come out!

"And finally, we have been on the rough seas of illness. Our crafts have been damaged. Now we are in the harbor and we drop anchor, attaching ourselves to a loving God. What a reassuring thought—*anchor in the spiritual.*

"Look at how the Creed ends," Maria continued. "Peace . . . God's peace . . . That is what we seek. There is real healing here on many levels.

"And the Creed closes with thankfulness, saying, 'Thank you, Lord, for today's blessings!' Being thankful is realizing and appreciating all we do have. We are blessed. On the journey to becoming triumphant, we want to express our appreciation and sincere gratitude for today's blessings.

"And there it is—a guide for wellness, a map for being triumphant, all packed into a powerful little creed."

The woman sat holding the necklace, looking at the inscription and thinking about all that Maria had said. A part of her wanted to abandon her skeptical, doubting nature and believe that hope does make a difference, that the world is a friendly place, and that a loving God really does exist.

But another part of her needed proof, hard evidence that this was more than an emotional placebo. After all, she was a woman of some intellect; she held a college degree; and she possessed years of experience from which she had learned to look at the world with discrimination.

Embracing what Maria and the Triumphant Patient had shared with her required not intellect or education or discrimination, but faith, childlike faith. The journey they were proposing was not based on rigorous scientific proof. It required faith, trust, and belief. It would be a spiritual journey.

It made her think of those childhood days when she was taught to submit to authority without questioning. It reminded her that she was told God would punish her if she did wrong. Was the same veiled threat behind all the Triumphant Patient and Maria were suggesting? She wasn't certain, but it seemed that's what she'd heard.

Finally, she spoke. "I'm not certain. I understand the need for an attitude of hope. But it is a long, long reach to connect that to the actual biology of my illness. For what you are saying to happen, our thoughts and emotions have to affect us on a cellular level. And that seems absurd."

"What seems absurd?" Maria asked.

"I believe the doctor. I know this is a serious illness. I know that my life will end rather soon, unless . . ."

The woman's voice trailed off, and the tears began. Weeping, she was finally able to whisper, "This whole situation is simply the worst thing I have ever experienced."

Maria waited until the weeping had subsided.

"I sense that you hold some common beliefs about illness and disability," she said. "But they are also probably untrue. Society has conditioned us to think very negatively about these issues. Some of that can be good. But much of it needs to be filtered through a process that helps us separate truth from untruth. I sense you are a person who would value such an exercise."

"I pride myself in my ability to understand the truth," the woman responded.

"Excellent," Maria said, "because what you believe about illness and wellness forms the foundation for much of the experience you will have. For a moment, think about this. There are three major untruths we are conditioned to believe about serious illness and disability:

"First, catastrophic illness or life-changing disability means death or a life of low quality.

"Second, treatment is ineffective and has bad side effects.

"Third, there is little patients can do to help themselves.

"These beliefs are all untrue. The truth about these three statements is:

"Illness or disability may or may not mean death or reduced life-quality.

"Treatment is becoming more effective and side effects less severe every day.

"There are many things patients can do—especially spiritually and psychologically—to help in their healing.

"The untruths tear at the very fiber of our hope and undermine everything we do. But the truths are grounded in reasonable hope. And that can be the difference, literally, between life and death.

"You said you pride yourself in analysis," Maria said. "Now, join me in a closer look at this powerful subject of beliefs."

The woman liked the way Maria put out this challenge to her. It was like exploring. And she was ready to explore.

"Okay," she said. "What do you have in mind?"

"Just this. Beliefs have two components. The Triumphant Patient calls these the 'mental' component and the 'emotional' component.

"Let's just take my situation as an example. When I was told I had multiple sclerosis, I developed a belief on two levels.

"One level was the mental."

Then Maria calmly, almost quietly said, "I have multiple sclerosis."

"The mental part of belief is actually an intellectual recognition that there is a problem. It comprehends on a rational, non-emotional level and assesses the situation in a logical, rather systematic manner.

"Do you understand belief on that level?" asked Maria.

"Of course," said the woman. "It is simply a recognition of the facts. It is what I did just a moment ago."

"That's it. But that was only a portion of my belief. There was another component. It was the emotional, and on the emotional level, the reaction was anything but rational. It was like this."

Maria got up from her chair, developed a panicked

expression on her face, and yelled at the top of her lungs, *"I HAVE MULTIPLE SCLEROSIS!!!"*

The force of Maria's voice was deafening, and the woman was startled. What was Maria going to do? Was she out of control? Had she gone crazy? Was Maria psychotic?

Maria saw the look of alarm on the woman's face.

"Don't be frightened," she said, smiling. "I allowed the dramatic to come out simply to make a point.

"Life-threatening illness generates tremendously powerful emotional responses. Those responses are the second, and the most powerful, part of the beliefs we hold. The problem is that many of those beliefs are untrue.

"These negative, adrenaline-charged false beliefs and emotions damage us physically, rob us of hope, lead to despair, and directly affect our ability to respond to our circumstances.

"When I heard 'multiple sclerosis,' the portion of the belief I had problems with was not the mental component. I rather easily took stock of the situation. My problem was the emotional component—the fear.

"I believed multiple sclerosis meant lingering debilitation, suffering, and death. But worse than that, I thought I might be incapacitated and unable to take care of myself. I would become an emotional and financial drain on family and friends for years to come. It was frightening, and it all stemmed from my beliefs about my condition.

"But when I changed my beliefs, I most assuredly changed my experience. And you can as well."

Could she? The woman was deep in thought. Might this really work for her? Could a challenge to her beliefs help her? She was so torn at times between her intellect and her intuition that years ago she decided not to trust her intuition.

"You want me to just change my beliefs, after having been told I am terminal? That's like lying to myself," she said.

Maria nodded her reassurance.

"I understand," she said. "I have been there too. For me, it was simple to believe the negative prognosis. I had multiple sclerosis. I would gradually become incapacitated and die.

"But then I realized that if I were to be triumphant, I'd need to start with the basic beliefs I held about my illness and my chance of recovery. I understood that I'd have to challenge the negative beliefs and assumptions of even my medical team. But I was determined I'd choose hope. And any beliefs that did not serve me well had to go.

"I want to be sure you clearly understand that *belief becomes biology.* Our responses to the world in which we live, touching off hope or fear, joy or despair, have a physical counterpart. This doesn't mean that medical treatment should be stopped in favor of positive beliefs. But it does mean that conventional medicine can be more effective when used in a comprehensive approach that includes positive beliefs."

This seemed logical to the woman and appealed to her reason.

"I understand," said the woman. "That makes a good deal of sense."

"I'm glad you agree," said Maria. "That is an important key. Do you also agree that accepting something on the intellectual level is not the same dynamic as believing? Belief mobilizes the powerful emotional component—either negatively, as in the case of fear, or positively, as in the case of hope."

Maria reached out and grasped the woman's arm.

"This is why I have spent so much time on the issues of beliefs and hope. It is absolutely critical to your wellness."

The woman could feel Maria's depth of concern and compassion.

"I want you to understand also that some will criticize you for adopting these beliefs," Maria said. "They'll say you did it in desperation, that you are clinging to false hope. But so far as the choice of hope has a biological reality, there is no such thing as false hope. There is simply hope.

"Perhaps the only false hope is the no hope some doctors falsely create with their negative prognoses.

"Taking away hope has a biological counterpart as well as a physical one. Your doctor said you are terminal. Except in the sense we will all die someday, that is a false statement. But in the perspective of your current illness, it is also an irresponsible statement."

"What do you mean?" asked the woman.

"Because only God can tell the outcome. And medical authorities who put themselves in this position have stepped outside the limits of their field of expertise."

"But my doctor told me I was terminal. He gave me a year. Are you saying he was wrong?" asked the woman.

"I am saying that what he told you was his opinion.

I am pointing out to you the truth—your illness may or may not mean death. And I am suggesting to you that your physician tore away a great deal of hope by telling you that in a year you will die.

"The answer to the question, 'How long do I have to live?' is the same for you as for everyone else, regardless of health. The real answer is, 'We don't know.'

"Instead of asking the question and then being terrified of the answer, I encourage you to believe that your illness may or may not mean death, that your treatment program will be effective, and that there is much you can do to help yourself in this situation. Those beliefs are dynamic and powerful, and they are filled with the promise of hope.

"Like the Triumphant Patient's Creed reminds us, these beliefs mean you can choose hope over despair and refuse to allow your illness to rule your life. While you acknowledge the physical, you can determine to be mentally positive, emotionally stable, and spiritually anchored in God's peace.

"The result is you can live this day, even with illness—in spite of illness—to the very fullest. You can enjoy its blessings. And that, my new friend, is more than many people, even without physical illness, do with their lives."

The woman was intrigued by these ideas.

"I have read that the body, the mind, and the spirit are related," she said, "and work together as one. The article said that the body can often respond physically to renewed feelings of hope."

"Yes," Maria said. "That's right. It's just what I've been trying to tell you. And all this little medallion does is remind us how to achieve it."

The woman was silent, thoughtful. Maria sensed it was time to let her be alone.

"Here's what I would like to see you do. Study the Creed this week, and practice what it suggests. And I will arrange an appointment for you next week with one of the most beautiful people you will ever meet. Her name is Susan. She has some thoughts to share with you on focusing the mind for healing, one of the most important wellness principles you will learn."

Maria made the call, and the time was set.

The woman referred to the Triumphant Patient's Creed and together she and Maria made notes to summarize their talk.

The Triumphant Patient's Positive Beliefs Summary

THE ILLNESS

- I do not believe life-threatening illness or disability is synonymous with death or low-quality living.

THE TREATMENT

- I establish a medical team in whom I have confidence.
- I believe my treatment program is effective.
- I believe the side effects, if any, can be managed.

MY ROLE

- There is much I can do to help in my own healing.
- I live today! Not yesterday. Not tomorrow. Today!
- I choose hope.

Chapter 4

FOCUS THE MIND FOR HEALING

"What was that? Would you say it again, please?"

The woman was confused and a little bit upset. If she'd heard correctly, Susan had just said, "You can be well if you just change your mind."

She'd been to see the Triumphant Patient, who had encouraged her to believe in the power of hope and take charge of her wellness. Next she'd gone to see Maria, who had spoken at length about beliefs. She said, "Belief becomes biology," and introduced the woman to the Triumphant Patient's Creed.

These ideas were very new to her, but after thinking about them and making notes in her journal, the woman found they were making a difference. She had begun to feel more hopeful, although at times the fear and despair would still wash over her. But once she had decided to try to live just for today, and not dwell on the past or be fearful of the future, her emotional state had improved. She didn't cry as often and she could love and enjoy her family again.

She'd had a long talk with her primary physician and told him that she wanted to know about her illness and participate in making decisions about her treatment. He had explained her illness more fully than before, and he told her why he ordered certain tests and what he expected to learn from them. When she summoned her courage and said she would like to have a second opinion, he said it was an excellent idea.

At home she had several books she'd checked out of a nearby library. Just going to the library to borrow them had been an accomplishment. But she hadn't begun to read them yet. She was still afraid of what she would learn.

All in all, she thought she'd made some progress, even though it wasn't much. Mentally and emotionally at least she'd begun to feel better and most days the things the Triumphant Patient and Maria had suggested to her were more on her mind than her illness.

Now she was visiting Susan. And Susan's words were just too much. She could be well if she just changed her mind? How could that be?

"I said, 'You can be *well* as quickly as it takes to change your mind,'" Susan repeated.

"Some who don't listen carefully think I have said anyone can be *cured* simply by changing his or her mind. Of course, that's not true. But we can be *well* by simply changing our minds. And anyone can do that."

Ah. She hadn't listened closely.

"But, wait," the woman thought. "*Cured* and *well*—don't they mean the same? Apparently they don't."

Susan was a tall woman with faultless posture.

There was about her an aura of dignity and serenity. The woman had been sitting in Susan's elegant but comfortable home office for some time while Susan told her story. And Susan's life did not match her attractive exterior.

Her husband, a well-known architect, had a dark side that for many years she had refused to acknowledge.

He was an alcoholic.

He was often sullen and withdrawn, and he rarely talked to Susan and their two children. Although he never actually struck anyone, he was abusive in other ways. He ridiculed Susan and the children, sometimes in front of their friends, and he was never satisfied with anything they did. They were constantly on edge, waiting to see what kind of mood he'd be in when he came home, whenever that might be. If he was angry or sullen, they tiptoed around him, trying to avoid upsetting him further. If he was in a rare pleasant mood, they tried to relax and enjoy it, knowing that at any moment the drink he almost always had in his hand when he was at home would take effect and his mood would suddenly change.

He was never responsible for anything that upset him. If anything was wrong, and usually something was, it was someone else's fault, most often Susan's. And believing she had responsibility for the well-being of her family, Susan would try to fix what was wrong. She constantly tried to adjust herself and the children to make him happy. But whatever she did, it was never enough. He said she was a lousy housekeeper, a terrible cook and hostess, and most of all a failure as a wife and mother.

They were part of the best social circles of their community and were frequently invited to dinners, parties, benefits, and other occasions, and they entertained often in their home. Susan's husband reminded her daily that the contacts he made during these affairs were important to his business. They had to be visible, he said, and make the right impression, so that when anyone wanted a building or an expensive house designed, they would contact him. "I'm the best!" he'd say. And he was very successful.

He'd tell her to "do something about your hair" and to buy a new dress. "You've gotta look good, Babe—like the wife of the state's number one architect!" He gave her expensive jewelry, and she always had an impressive car to drive, although he rarely consulted her before he made a purchase. He insisted that she serve on boards and be active in community affairs. At parties she would hear him speak of "my wife" with pride as he described her activities. Those were the only times he acknowledged or complimented her. In a way it made her feel good and she would try even harder to live up to his expectations.

She did enjoy their social life. At a party her husband was friendly and witty—the center of attention. He could talk on almost any subject and always appeared to be knowledgeable. The other guests seemed to be drawn to him, listening to his jokes, asking his advice, enjoying his company. It was fun and Susan always had a good time until it was time to go home.

By then he was drunk and she didn't want him to drive them home. They always had a fight about who would drive. He thought allowing his wife to drive was a mark against his manhood. Those were the only arguments she ever won. He'd give in only when she refused to get in the car if he drove. She'd say, "Wrap yourself around a telephone pole if you want to, but I won't let you take me with you. I'll call a cab." Then finally he'd give her the car keys.

She talked herself into thinking she had a good life. She knew her husband's drinking was out of control, but she believed that one day he would wake up, realize what he was doing to himself and their family, and stop. Then everything would be fine—if she could just hold on long enough for it to happen.

She didn't sleep well and she usually had a headache in the morning. Eating breakfast made her sick, so she waited until noon to eat. She drank coffee until the headaches went away. Two or three times a year she got a pinched nerve in her back and spent three or four days suffering in bed until the inflammation was gone. She developed a blood sugar problem and often suffered sudden dizziness. Her stomach was usually tied in knots and the tension was so great in her shoulders and neck that touching her there actually hurt.

"My life was making me sick," Susan said. "And I wasn't just a little under the weather. I became more and more ill until several times a week I couldn't get up in the morning. It would be noon or the middle of the afternoon before I would feel well enough to get dressed. The dizzy spells, the headaches, the nausea all got worse and I began to have constant indigestion. I ate antacid tablets by the handful.

"Then one day I had stabbing chest pains. It was excruciating. The pain spread across my chest and down one arm. I became feverish and finally collapsed.

"With barely enough strength to crawl to my telephone, I dialed the emergency number and called for an ambulance. It wasn't long before I lay in a hospital unit hooked up to countless monitors. They said I'd had a heart attack, and they said it was a serious one. The doctors weren't certain yet, but they believed there was a strong possibility of permanent damage.

"A heart attack at fifty-two years of age! I couldn't believe it. Not me. This must be a bad dream, I thought. How could I have a heart attack? Why I was practically indestructible. But as the panic subsided and I lay there in that hospital for two weeks, I began to reflect. Eventually it occurred to me that perhaps I shouldn't have been surprised.

"I began to see a relationship between a life that had gone off course and a heart that had done the same, and I took some important time to reflect. I made the connection that if I addressed the problems in my life, perhaps the problems of my heart would be relieved."

Susan was intelligent and articulate and sophisticated. The woman sensed she had an outstanding education. But she had more than knowledge; she was also wise. And she was saying that negative conditions in her life were a factor in the negative conditions of her health.

But she hadn't stopped there. She was saying that if her life conditions could be changed, there might be a change in her health at the same time. In Susan's educated judgment, at least, there was a correlation. This was another new idea, and it seemed worth exploring.

"So what did you do?" the woman asked.

"I began to seriously explore the idea of changing my mind. Oh, I carefully followed my doctors' advice. I changed my diet to eat healthily and I began a supervised exercise program. I began to do something about my compulsive codependent behaviors too. But the most important change I needed to make was to get control of my mind—my very thoughts and emotions. I began to look inside myself to better understand the way I had been living my life.

"I'd been pulling the psychological covers over my head for years. I pushed my fear and anger against my husband down very deep. That takes a lot of energy and results in tremendous resentment.

"Certainly my diet and exercise habits were not the best and they contributed to my ill health. But the psychological and emotional issues had set up a vicious cycle, and they kept it going. I had to get off that merry-go-round of self-destruction. So I undertook a program to change my mind."

"Did you think that your mind caused your illness? Did you have a psychosomatic heart attack?" the woman asked.

"Does the word *psychosomatic* have a derogatory meaning for you?" Susan responded.

"Yes," said the woman. "A doctor once told me that my son's asthma was all in his mind. And as soon as he left home for college, his problems did clear up."

"Interesting," said Susan. "So you see the mind as being able to create health problems, is that correct?"

"Yes."

"If the mind can create health problems, then would it be likely that the mind and spirit are also able to create health solutions?" Susan asked.

"When you put it that way, I suppose so. But I've always thought of psychosomatic as referring to imagining illness that doesn't really exist," the woman said.

"The word *psychosomatic* derives from two Greek

words," Susan said, "*psyche* and *soma*, which mean 'mind, or soul,' and 'body.' When the word originated, it was meant to convey the potential for the relationship between body, mind, and soul positively as well as negatively. The way you have understood the meaning is only part of the negative potential.

"It's possible for someone to imagine an illness for the purpose of getting attention, for example, and then begin to produce symptoms. It is also possible for a person to *believe* he or she is sick, when there is no medical evidence of illness, and believe it so strongly that he or she would actually become sick and have serious symptoms.

"For example, a woman believed so strongly that she was pregnant, her mind directed a whole series of physical changes in her body. Hormone activity increased, her breasts enlarged, menstruation ceased, she experienced morning sickness, and eventually she even began to have labor contractions."

"You're talking about a false pregnancy, aren't you?" the woman asked.

"In the sense that there was no fertilized egg or growing fetus, yes, it was a false pregnancy, at least in the way modern medicine would define a pregnancy. But her body responded as if she were pregnant."

The woman was quiet and thoughtful. What did this really mean to her? She certainly had not convinced herself that she was seriously ill and would die, nor had she imagined or believed it. The thoughts had never occurred to her until her doctor told her.

"The mind can also effectively control pain," Susan continued. "This can be accomplished by the simple mental discipline of concentrating on other sensations. I have seen people walk on hot coals or sleep on beds of nails. And although I certainly do not recommend these practices, we must admit that they can be done. These people employ their minds in those efforts.

"Another very interesting example of the power of the mind is the shaman of primitive cultures. The shaman was a priest who used magic for the purpose of curing the sick. And often the sick got well after he had cast his spell on them. Some shamans also used a technique called *boning*. The shaman would point a 'magical' bone at a person accused of a wrongdoing. The person would writhe in pain and often died within a few hours. The shaman's power was in the power of suggestion, based wholly in the mind of the accused, who believed very strongly that if the shaman pointed the magical bone at him, he would die. His belief was the only physical cause of his death.

"There is an occult part of this phenomenon that greatly disturbs me," Susan said. "But it is another demonstration of the power of the mind and spirit and how it can work so forcefully."

The woman shook her head. Yes, she had heard these stories before. But they were quite difficult to believe.

"This is modern day civilization," countered the woman. "Surely we have come a long way from believing in the power of a stick or a handful of powder sprinkled over someone's head."

Susan nodded. "I agree. But the principles behind these experiences can apply to life today. Ministers, priests, and rabbis have been teaching about them for centuries. Now modern medical research, after long study, is finally beginning to put its stamp of approval on the mind/body/spirit principles as practical and effective.

"In a recent study, for example, breast cancer patients who took part in a weekly support group session had a survival rate more than twice that of another group who did not participate. Research today simply confirms the realities of these ancient truths. The mind and spirit have a powerful role in wellness. And you can use your mind to help in your healing.

"We can put our mental and spiritual assets to work to help us. And as we learn better how to manage these assets, we allow our bodies these valuable resources to fight illness."

"It all seems so unscientific," the woman responded.

Susan observed the woman. There she was again, doubting and resisting. But maybe her doubts actually were cries for help, coming from someone who was frightened and greatly in need. Susan believed that was the case.

"Please, be more open to this," Susan said. "No one is asking you to mindlessly follow a set of beliefs and actions that have no basis in fact. Some may not have the scientific proof you seem to want, but they do have the wisdom of the ages.

"There are three revolutionary thoughts I'd like you to consider to see what they might mean to you.

"First, *we feel the way we think.*

"Do you believe that we feel the way we think?"

"I'm not certain," said the woman. "What does it mean?"

"It means that the manner in which we cognitively process the events of our lives, whether good or bad, is the way we will experience life. This is not convoluted logic. It is simply a recognition of the fact that we perceive an event or circumstance and then generate a feeling, or an emotional response, from that perception.

"As a simple example: You get up in the morning, find it is raining, and say, 'I can't do the yard work today because it's raining.' And you go about the day feeling depressed. Or, you get up, see the same rain, and think, 'What a break! This gives me a chance to catch up on my reading.' And you have a wonderful day. It's the same day, but we've considered two different ways of thinking about it.

"You see, in a real sense, we do feel the way we think."

The woman smiled. "Yes, I can accept that."

"The second principle is: *Thought is the ancestor of every life experience.*

"Thought precedes experience, and no matter what the experience, the thought we have toward it will determine our experience.

"In another example, let's say that after a hectic day you put your child to bed. Now it is your turn to sit down and relax. Twenty minutes later he opens the door to his room and walks out giggling. Your reaction might be, 'That kid never gives me a moment's peace.' Or you might react by thinking, 'This is good. Now he can crawl out of his bed on his own. He's learning independence.'

"It's the same situation with two different experiences based solely on how you thought about the situation. Thought is the ancestor of every life experience."

"I can think of a life experience thought does not influence," said the woman.

"What is that?" asked Susan.

"What about our involuntary nervous systems? That is a life experience that thought does not affect."

"But subconscious thought is in control there too. We know that our minds control those body functions, and we understand that they control them without our conscious efforts.

"Have you heard of biofeedback?" Susan asked.

"I've heard the term," the woman answered, "but I actually know little about it."

"Through biofeedback people can train themselves to direct and control body processes that were previously thought to be involuntary. Specialists now know how an individual can direct blood pressure, heart rate, and brain waves, and can even vary the temperature in his or her hands. We can do it through the power of our minds by imagining that something is so, and it is.

"So even our anatomical nervous systems, if not controlled by our conscious minds, are under the direction of the subconscious. Thought and the mind. Truly they are the ancestors of every single life experience."

"Are they the ancestors of illness too?" asked the woman.

"They are the ancestors of our experiences of illness," Susan responded. "For example, two people are given the very same diagnosis. For one it is tragedy, the worst possible nightmare, a certain sign of the end of life.

"But for the other person, the illness is more a challenge than a threat. It is a call to begin a new and better life, recapturing the dreams that for years perhaps have been put on hold.

"The difference between the two responses is thought, the ancestor of every life experience."

The woman considered what Susan had just said. It made some sense, but she was resistant. It seemed to mean that she had made herself sick and she couldn't stand thinking that somehow she was responsible, even if she'd done something unknowingly. But then that really wasn't what Susan was talking about. She was talking about the way a person responds to illness. That is different and that she could think about.

This whole triumphant journey challenged her every moment. The Triumphant Patient hadn't warned her about that. He hadn't told her that constantly she would be stretched, that her every assumption would be questioned. It was exhausting, but she was getting a new perspective.

She looked up at Susan. "You said there are three revolutionary beliefs. What is number three?"

"The third belief is: *What we think about expands.*

"What we give our thought energy to tends to be our life experience. It grows.

"Thoughts held in the mind become expectations. And we tend to move along the line of our expectations. We tend to experience what we believe we will experience, what we plan to experience, what we prepare ourselves to experience. This is true not only on a health level, but in all areas of life.

"If we expect to experience a troubled relationship and we look for fault in others, we will probably find more than enough fault to justify our expectations.

"But we could just as well look for good qualities. And if we look, we will discover an abundance of reasons to justify our expectations of goodness."

"Yes, I understand," said the woman, "but what in the world does that have to do with getting well?"

"It has very much to do with getting well!" Susan responded. "We can choose our responses to any experience, holding before us expectations of hope and wellness or illness and despair. We will then tend to move along the lines of those expectations.

"And what we think about does expand. As it relates to illness, our expectations of experiencing the best or the worst determine a large measure of that reality.

"A perfect example of how this works happened recently. A woman who was going through cancer called me. It was obvious from the start of the call that she had let her mind get out of control with many fears.

"After just a few minutes on the phone, I began to jot down the first words of her sentences. Read this aloud," Susan said as she handed the woman a page of handwritten notes, "and notice how this person's mind was affecting her well-being."

The woman took the paper and began to read.

"I get sore when I have to just lie here . . .

"It hurts when I try to move . . .

"I can no longer lift the walker . . .

"My bone marrow is 'low' . . .

"It's all such a burden . . .

"My insurance might be canceled . . .

"I'm in so much pain . . .

"I don't know what's ahead . . .

"I'm afraid of radiation . . .

"I'm confined to bed most of the time . . .

"It's all so painful . . .

"I'm so afraid . . .

"My cancer is spreading . . .

"My cancer is playing hide-and-seek . . .

"I've had to work so hard . . .

"I'm a driven person . . .

"My life has been very difficult . . .

"I've never had someone who was really for me . . .

"My husband was self-centered . . .

"My self-esteem is low . . .

"I have no self-confidence . . .

"I cry all the time . . .

"Every time they bring food, I cry . . .

"I'm so helpless . . ."

The woman looked at Susan. "This is incredible. Surely you made it up."

"I wish that were the case," Susan said, "but I didn't. Those are her words. Her mind was working so much against her well-being that it is a wonder she was even alive.

"We all contribute to our demise when we allow our minds to run like that. We call it 'awfulizing,' meaning we think the worst possible outcomes will befall us. And awfulizing can and will affect us in body, mind, and spirit."

The woman was thoughtful. "That example makes a pretty obvious point," she said. "I can see the connection.

"We can choose our mental responses, can't we?"

Susan was pleased with that comment.

"Exactly. We can control our thought processes and hold in mind those thoughts that will contribute to our wellness, not to our demise. Scientists have verified that the positive choices of gratitude, inner peace, love, hope, happiness, support of friends, joy have great effects on people.

"I believe that a person who is at peace and surrounded by loving support heals better. Clearly he or she has an improved quality of life. And I believe from my personal experience that this has the added effect of allowing the body's healing mechanisms to perform to their maximum."

The woman seemed receptive to Susan's teaching, nodding her head with understanding.

"The more we understand about the relationship between the body, the mind, and the spirit, the more difficult it is to separate them," Susan said. "We must soon conclude that anything that delivers hope has the potential to move us toward wellness. And this has significant meaning for us."

"What does it mean we should do?" asked the woman. "How then do we live?"

Again Susan was pleased with the woman's response. She was so very perceptive. If she could just be persuaded to give these principles a chance to work in her life, surely she would benefit.

"This all means that we can use our minds in our own healing efforts. And we can do so in two distinct ways.

"First, we can calm our minds. Think of the woman's comments that you just read. Her mind had her in the grip of fear-filled terror and self-pity. But there was something she could do. She was a victim of that thought process only as long as she allowed it. She could have calmed her mind and thus improved her entire well-being."

"How?" asked the woman.

"Through prayer and meditation. Instead of allowing her mind to awfulize negative after negative, she could calm her mind voluntarily, deliberately. Actually she could choose her thoughts.

"The Triumphant Patient teaches a simple meditation technique that thousands of people have found helpful."

"Meditation?" the woman exclaimed. "Oh no! I've seen some strange-looking people doing that sort of thing, sitting in weird positions, wearing ridiculous clothing. I'm not going to do any thing like that. I'm not about to meditate."

Susan was surprised at the woman's rather strong reaction, but perhaps this was simply another cry for help. Susan was determined to respond with compassion.

"I fully understand your feelings. I felt some of the same when I began my triumphant journey. But then I came to value meditation as a workable technique that could bring me peace of mind. And I was quite willing to give up my preconceived notions about it in exchange for some peace of mind. One thing you might remember is that we don't meditate in public. We don't do it for show. If you should decide to meditate, you'd do it in the privacy of your home. The Triumphant Patient recommends meditating as a way to achieve peace of mind.

"How do you feel about peace of mind? Is that something you would like to have?"

"Well, yes. Of course," responded the woman. "But I just can't see myself meditating."

"Please, explore this technique with me for just five minutes. I promise, we won't have you looking strange, dressing weirdly, or sitting with your legs crossed," smiled Susan.

"Okay." The woman giggled softly. Susan, like Maria and the Triumphant Patient, was so sincere. She obviously believed this technique would help, so why not try it? Why not spend five minutes thinking about it?

"Let's try to understand how meditating might help in your healing," Susan said. "And how you would actually do it if you decided to try it.

"First, you'll want to find a quiet place where you can physically relax. I use this home office where we are sitting. In fact, when I need time alone, I hang a sign on the outside doorknob. My family knows they are to respect my request, and they don't interrupt unless it's an emergency. And they really don't interrupt. Since they've noticed the positive changes my alone times have had in me, they not only don't interrupt, they are very supportive. And they even asked me to show them how they could do it.

"You know, I wasn't the only one in my family who was angry and afraid and resentful. The way I was living my life—pushing my emotions down deep, constantly filled with negative stress and tension—was a powerful role model for my children. And then they had another very powerful role model too, their alcoholic father.

"My heart attack was a significant challenge for them as well as for me. Their first thoughts were that they wanted me to get my life back on track. They wanted me to be well. They wanted me to live. As they watched me take those first halting, timid steps, and began to see the results, they encouraged me. Then they began to think about themselves. Eventually, they decided to change their minds too. Now both the children meditate every day."

"What about your husband?" the woman asked.

"Ah, my husband," Susan said, a look of sadness briefly crossing her face. "One of the things you must remember about the journey to becoming triumphant is that we each choose to make the journey. No one can make us do it, and no one can make the journey for us.

"He hasn't decided yet to become triumphant."

"I'm sorry," the woman said quietly. "I didn't mean to pry or to bring up a negative."

"That's quite all right," Susan said. "It's important to realize we are each responsible for ourselves. His inaction will not determine my wellness."

"Then let's get back to our discussion of meditating," the woman said. "All of a sudden I find that I want to know more. I'm beginning to think that I would like to change my mind."

Susan smiled and said, "As I was saying, I hang out my sign to signal my family that I need some time alone and I sit in this chair. Then I relax, physically. I just sit. Some people get in the lotus position, others kneel, some stand and sway, some even prostrate themselves on the floor. Those ways are all fine, but like most meditators, I prefer to sit. And then I relax.

"I relax my muscles throughout my body, particularly across the shoulders and up the neck. That is the tension triangle where we physically carry much of our emotional stress. Just try that now."

Susan paused for a few minutes while the woman attempted to relax her body.

"Next I choose a focus word, actually a focus phrase. And I use one that is consistent with and meaningful to my religious beliefs. I use a phrase from Psalm 23: 'The Lord is my shepherd.' I suggest you also choose something that has meaning to you spiritually."

"Well, I'm not a churchgoer," said the woman.

"Then how about a neutral word. What about something like 'peace'; would that be acceptable?"

"Peace. Yes, that's good. Peace."

"Wonderful. This simple word will be of great help to you in attaining peace of mind.

"Next I close my eyes and start repeating the word or phrase silently each time I breathe out. For example, slowly breathe in and out. As your breath goes out, say 'peace' silently to yourself. Breathe in, breathe out, 'peace.' In, out, 'peace.'

"As you continue, you will notice that distracting thoughts may keep coming into your mind. The mind is an active entity, always at work. You'll be aware of this mental chatter, this thought bombardment. Simply take a passive attitude toward these intrusions. Observe them and let them go. They just don't matter right now. Don't be concerned with them. Don't try to force them out of your mind. Just dismiss them by returning to your focus word or phrase. Continue to breathe in silently and breathe out while silently repeating the focus word."

"That is all very interesting," said the woman, "and seems quite simple and easy to do. But just what am I supposed to get out of it?"

"The benefit is a mind that is calm and is not holding you hostage like our friend's was," Susan answered. "And this certainly aids in your total well-being.

"As you continue meditating for ten or twenty minutes at a time, you'll experience a peacefulness you didn't have before. And this peacefulness will stay with you for a period of time, contributing to your well-being.

"Now you have a technique to use to put you back in control when your mind is racing with fears and anxieties. For once your mind won't be churning through a list of things it needs to be happy. It won't be focused on what is wrong or how badly the doctor treated you or how much pain you are in or how frightening the illness is or . . .

"The list of things a mind can worry about goes on and on. Our minds are overactive when it comes to responding to adversity. Stress, suffering, no peace of mind are all common reactions. Meditation is a technique to bring those reactions under our control and to focus our minds for healing."

"Those are truly some significant benefits," said the woman.

"After you have meditated for ten to twenty minutes, take a moment to picture your illness as you see it physically in your body. Or give it a symbol. Then imagine your own body and its wondrous healing capabilities eliminating the disease in a natural way. If you are taking medication or having treatment, imagine it assisting your body's naturally powerful abilities.

"End the meditation period by imagining yourself

full of radiant health, smiling and happy to be alive."

"I was with you until now. That sounds a little like quackery to me," said the woman. "It seems foolish. I can't imagine how that could possibly work."

"If that is how you feel, then you shouldn't do it," replied Susan. "Just know that thousands of others do have strong belief in imagery and have found it helpful. If it is not right for you now, it may be at another time. But I do hope you will take time to meditate twice a day for ten to twenty minutes at a time."

"That part does make sense," responded the woman. "I look forward to trying it."

"Would you care to close our session with a meditation?" Susan asked.

"Yes, I would."

"Then, allow me to quietly lead you," said Susan.

She went to the door and put out her sign.

"Now, just sit in a comfortable position, and relax. Let's relax our muscles from toe to head. And I almost always gently close my eyes to keep out distractions.

"First tense the muscles. And then just let them relax. Let's start with the toes. Curl the toes. And let them relax."

Susan paused and they both completed the exercise.

"Next, let's tense our legs. And then gently relax.

"Now, we'll make a fist and tense the muscles in our arms. Now relax and let go. Let your arms just lie in your lap.

"Tense your shoulders and neck. This is the tension triangle, across the shoulders and up into the neck, where we carry so much of our stress. First tense and then relax.

"Finally, clench your jaw and contract the muscles in your forehead. Now relax. Allow your jaws to be comfortably apart and make sure your tongue is off the roof of your mouth, and relax.

"Already you are feeling more peaceful.

"Using your focus word, *peace*, we'll become aware of our breathing. We'll breathe in silently and on the out breath repeat silently to ourselves the word *peace*. Just continue this," whispered Susan. "Breathe in silently. Breathe out with the word *peace*.

"When a distracting thought comes," whispered Susan, "just gently dismiss it and return to your breathing and the focus word *peace*."

The two women sat silently for about fifteen minutes, each enjoying this time of meditation.

Finally Susan said quietly, "Now, I would like you to open your eyes and feel the peace."

The woman opened her eyes and smiled. There was a pleasant serenity that she had not felt before.

"This is what meditation can do for you. And this is the way you can focus the mind for healing."

The woman thanked Susan for all her time and help, and as soon as she arrived home she sat down to make notes.

Focusing the Mind for Healing

- I can become well as quickly as I change my mind.
- I feel the way I think.
- Thought is the ancestor of every life experience.
- What I think about expands.
- I can control my "awfulizing."
- Twice a day I will meditate. I'll—
  Find a quiet place and relax.
  Choose a focus word.
  Repeat the focus word with my breathing.
  Gently dismiss distractions and return to the focus word.
  Continue for ten to twenty minutes.

Chapter 5

THE HEALING POWER OF FORGIVENESS

W hen the woman left Susan, she had a great deal to think about. She'd been very resistant to the idea of meditating, but after listening to Susan talk about changing and calming her mind in order to have peace of mind, she was willing to try it. She did want to be peaceful. She remembered her reaction after her doctor told her about her illness—all that raging and crying and self-pity were exhausting. Then she got very honest with herself, and she knew she didn't want to do those things any more. She truly wanted to be peaceful.

After meditating with Susan at the end of their talk, the feeling of serenity lasted several hours, until in the supermarket parking lot another customer stole the parking space she was waiting for. She had a sudden rush of anger and felt it was a personal affront. Then she remembered slights from other people until her mood turned dark.

After dinner that evening, she asked her family not to disturb her, went into her bedroom, and spent twenty minutes quietly breathing in, breathing out, and repeating "peace" until the peacefulness returned. Since then she had meditated twice a day. The new sense of calm she felt was wonderful except that something would happen or someone would say something that struck her wrong and she'd quickly get angry. She didn't understand why that happened. She wanted to be serene. Maybe she just needed more practice.

At first she'd thought relaxation was the purpose of meditation. But in time she realized that the primary benefit was awareness. As she repeated her focus word, she began to observe and identify her thoughts, and gradually she was able to choose her thoughts. She realized that Susan was right. What we think about does expand.

Then she began to consider the other two principles Susan had taught her: *Thought is the ancestor of every life experience*, and *we feel the way we think*.

She'd learned early in life that there were things that upset her. She felt that at those times some kind of response was legitimate. Some people were rude, others were unkind, still others were dishonest. She believed anger was justified in those situations. People needed to know when they were wrong. Otherwise they'd never learn to improve themselves.

She did get angry when those situations occurred. Had she decided in advance to be angry? No, she didn't think she had. She was merely reacting to situations based on her past experiences. Isn't that the wise thing to do? It seems foolish not to learn from experience.

Edward had called and introduced himself as the next person the Triumphant Patient wanted her to meet. They agreed to get together in the park. She arrived a little early and waited for him with anticipation, eager to know what new principle of wellness he would reveal. The day was warm and sunny, and the park grounds were beautiful. She felt safe there, emotionally safe as well as physically safe. She enjoyed the trees and the flowers and the wildlife, and she wondered why she hadn't enjoyed the park more often.

As she waited she reflected more on the benefits of meditating and particularly on choosing her thoughts. She'd discovered that although some times she could choose her thoughts, at other times she couldn't. Some experiences seemed to nag at her, and she couldn't let go of the memory of them. She'd had a minor confrontation with her husband that morning and, even though she'd been right to respond in the way she had, somehow she couldn't get that experience out of her mind. It continued to pop up without warning. If she could just get rid of the memory of it, the day would be perfect. Since it had been a minor disagreement and she had resolved it, she didn't know why the memory was still so fresh.

She and her husband were having breakfast together, and they were each reading different sections of the paper. He was reading the local news section where he found an article about someone he knew, a business acquaintance. Without a word to her, he tore out the article, folded it, and put it in his pocket.

She said, "What are you doing? I haven't read that part yet."

And he said, "Sorry, hon. It's just something I wanted to take to the office. I'll bring it home tonight and you can read it then."

That made her mad. He was so thoughtless. She shook her head as she remembered it. He knew she'd let him read that section first, but he'd made a big hole in one of the pages. She had to remind him that was thoughtless and she pointed out how she always tried to be thoughtful of him. But he just looked at her and didn't say anything.

Then she'd reminded him of other times he'd been thoughtless. But still he didn't answer. That was when she was actually angry with him because he didn't say anything to let her know he understood. She'd explained it all to him again. He really needed to learn not to ruin the paper until others have read it.

Finally he understood and acknowledged his mistake. He took the clipping out of his pocket, laid it on the table, said, "I'll buy another paper on the way into town," and left. She was free to enjoy the paper, but she couldn't. It was ruined, and every time she saw the hole in the paper, she felt fresh anger. She remembered the other times he'd made holes in the paper. Then she thought of other times he'd been thoughtless and times he hadn't taken her advice and consequently made a serious mistake and times he'd just been wrong.

Eventually she was quite upset. She even began to tremble and her stomach was tied in knots. She felt one of her headaches coming on. She meditated for thirty minutes before she could calm her mind. But that hole in the paper wouldn't go away, and it was bothering her still.

Why? she wondered. Could she possibly have gotten so upset over the morning paper? Wasn't that a little silly? It wasn't the paper, was it? It was all the other things she remembered because of the paper.

She resolved to think about this more. Obviously there was something else she needed to understand.

She saw Edward approaching and she turned her thoughts to him in anticipation of what he would tell her.

He was a tall, gentle man, articulate, refined, and confident, and a perfect gentleman. She felt at ease with him and found his serenity especially appealing. He seemed the picture of wellness, and immediately she was curious about his journey.

"I've not learned all perhaps I should have in my seventy-four years," Edward said. "But there are a few things that stand out. One is that life can be lived most abundantly as an adventure in forgiveness.

"Nothing clutters the soul more than resentment, remorse, and recrimination. These emotions, based in anger and guilt, occupy a fearsome amount of space in our minds. They block our experiences and drain our lives of joy and peace. They lead us to hate and hate is death."

The woman could sense Edward's depth of understanding. He spoke with the compassion of someone who had actually made a triumphant journey. But could Edward—quiet, dignified, serene Edward— have done battle with hate? He seemed the last person who would have that trouble.

"Forgiveness," he said, "is the key that opens the

lock of hate—forgiveness of ourselves and of others.

"Forgiveness frees us from the self-punishment and emotional investment that hate demands, and it demands a heavy price. Forgiveness allows us to live a life of triumph, free from the bondage of guilt and grudge."

"I think I agree that hate is bad and forgiveness is good," she said, "but I don't see much relationship between hate and death. Are you saying that hate causes physical illness?"

"I'm saying that hate is death and forgiveness is life."

"Can you put that in more everyday terms? Do you mean a person who hates, who really hates, misses the good things in life and therefore isn't really alive?" she asked.

"A person who is bound up in hate does miss the good things in life," Edward said. "But it's much more than that.

"Nothing contaminates us more than resentment, remorse, and recrimination. These emotions do more to stand in the way of our wellness than virtually any other issues. And they do not develop only because of catastrophic or crushing events. We often feel them in response to the minor, everyday events of life."

An image of the morning paper flashed into the woman's mind. Instantly she understood. She had allowed resentment to build. Subconsciously she'd actually remembered every single thing about her husband that she didn't like, that hurt her feelings, or that seemed not to be respectful of her and her opinions. It was as though she had been keeping a record. Then she'd brought all of that back and unloaded it because of a minor irritation. Now she was feeling guilty. How does one avoid that?

"But there is a way out of this trap," Edward said. "It is the pathway of forgiveness.

"Actually we tend to forget major events and trivial hurts rather than to forgive them. But forgetting and forgiving are not the same. When we forget, we are not really finished with these issues. They only come back later to haunt us and demand resolution. Once we have forgiven, though, we then have new perspectives for forgetting, a healthy sign that puts trivial as well as major events behind us. Once forgiven, we can handle these events with integrity because we have been healed."

The woman was quiet for several minutes.

"I think I understand what you are saying," she said. "But I'm not sure I can see a connection between forgiving and illness. Not forgiving wouldn't cause an illness, would it?"

"In attempting to answer your question, I want to tell you my story," Edward said. "And I'd like you to consider if the things I learned about myself could be partially true of you.

"At one time in my life," he began, "I was a severely critical and condemning person. I set myself up as judge and jury. I always had to be right. And if I was right, of course, others were wrong.

"If you think about that kind of behavior, you will soon see how much time and emotional energy it consumes," Edward said.

"What do you mean you always had to be right?" the woman asked.

"This is an important point of wellness," Edward

said. "For me it was an issue of perception. I was so concerned with what other people thought of me, I rarely considered that I might be wrong. I needed everyone to know that I was right, to acknowledge that I always had the right answers.

"Actually, though, my self-image was weak, and I was afraid that if I was wrong, others would realize I wasn't perfect. Therefore, I *had* to be right. I elevated my simple opinions to gospel truth. I needed to have everyone recognize that my version of the truth was the only correct position to hold. I was also very thorough in considering others' actions and problems and concerns and could quite easily determine what they should do, how they should behave, and what they should think. I viewed my main task in life as sitting on a stool and handing out critical advice."

The woman smiled at Edward's exaggeration. Still it was difficult to picture him being judgmental or arrogant or impressed with himself. And she really couldn't imagine him meddling.

"Then I began constantly doing something that was even worse," he continued. "I became a critic. It followed so naturally. If I was always right, then those whose point of view differed from mine were obviously wrong. But I didn't stop with just labeling them as wrong, I condemned them as being stupid. And I became eager to tell them so.

"I convinced myself I was intellectually and morally superior. I was arrogance personified, topped off with a critical cynicism that made me unapproachable. When I said I was being frank with people, I was actually judging them, for I always needed to be right. I realize now how revolting I was."

The woman was beginning to feel a little uncomfortable. She was usually quite good at seeing others' faults and had always felt a responsibility to share her insight. Was Edward suggesting that was being judgmental? No, she didn't think so. She was certain that pointing out people's errors was being helpful, not judgmental.

"Of course," Edward said, "I didn't realize the tremendous emotional price one has to pay to assume and maintain these positions. And at the emotional level is where this attitude and behavior of always having to be right affects one's health. It led me deeper into resentment and recrimination.

"It was insidious behavior on my part," he continued.

"Around those people I felt were only marginally important to me, I responded to any criticism of my positions by saying something cutting, like 'How long has blissful ignorance served you so well?'

"In front of those I knew best, even those I loved, I often exploded. I'd become enraged and was verbally and emotionally abusive to the very people I loved most. I would become infused with anger at those in my closest circle who dared challenge me.

"But the most physically damaging times were when I perceived a challenge to my position and felt I couldn't respond. Usually that was when I was challenged by the people I wanted to look good for, the ones I most wanted to impress.

"The emotions were wrenching. But, needing to impress, I couldn't allow myself to explode the way I often did in front of my closest friends and family. I had to hold the emotions in. That's when I burned with resentment at others or at circumstances. The resentment tormented me, and I sank farther into the abyss of insecurity and contempt."

Edward closed his eyes and covered them briefly with his hand, then looked ahead toward some children playing. When he spoke again, his voice was barely audible.

"I'm not proud of this behavior," he said. "When I think of all the people I hurt, I am so sorry. And when I think of what this behavior did to me, there is no doubt in my mind that it was an integral part of my testing positive for the HIV virus."

Edward's confession stunned the woman. He seemed the essence of the gentle, caring person, someone who was not quick to criticize or become angry, one who would give anyone a second chance. And it was interesting what listening to his confession did to her. At first she found herself judging him. Then she began to see herself in his story. Finally she wanted to extend her compassion to him.

They sat quietly for a time. The woman thought about Edward and, although she couldn't see that she had been quite so arrogant and unkind as he, she could find in her behavior some similarities to his. The realization made her feel icy inside.

She had always thought of her own critical nature and impatience as justifiable and appropriate. She held onto it tenaciously. She wanted to remember the hurts. If someone criticized or wronged her, and she didn't remember it, then the incident wouldn't be important and the offender would be free to hurt her again. No one should let that happen.

"What did you do?" she asked.

"I discovered I did not know how to forgive," Edward answered.

"Forgive?"

"Yes. Forgive. My illness was directing me to confront my inability to forgive. And as I began to examine this issue, I also began to realize its direct link to my wellness. As I learned to forgive, I became well."

"Who did you forgive?" she asked.

"Everyone," Edward answered.

"Everyone? Regardless of what they'd done?"

"Yes."

"But some people don't deserve to be forgiven," she said.

"That may be true."

"What did you do about them?" she asked.

"I forgave them."

The woman looked long and hard at Edward.

"Is that what I am supposed to learn from you today?" she asked.

"Yes," he answered.

"Everyone?" she asked again.

"Yes, everyone," he responded.

She looked away, shaking her head. "I can't," she said. "I won't. There are some things that shouldn't be forgiven—*can't* be forgiven! Not ever!"

To prove her point she began to tell Edward about a former co-worker who had done wrong to her, a wrong so inexcusable it could not possibly be forgiven. As she recounted each aspect of her betrayal, her face darkened, her body tensed, and her voice took on the hardness of hate. She let go. All hints of serenity drained from her face. She stood and began to pace back and forth in front of Edward, wringing her hands and balling them into fists. As the recital built to a crescendo, tears filled her eyes.

The woman was consumed by the drama. She paced, talked, and pointed her finger. Then the floodgates burst. She cried as the torrent of resentment poured out. When she finished with her co-worker, she went on to describe others—business associates, friends, family, casual acquaintances. Edward observed an attractive woman transformed into something ugly. Not since his own experience had he witnessed such vehemence.

There were those in her own family against whom she had built walls of resentment—her husband, her parents, even one of her children. At one point remembering these feelings was so painful she screamed, "I just hate them." And then more tears fell.

Edward was calm and filled with compassion. Without judging her, he observed the woman's tremendous investment of energy in these issues. He could plainly see that she needed always to be right, and what this was doing to her, not just to her health, but to her entire well-being and her whole life.

When she seemed to be finished, he asked, "Is that all?"

Then she remembered something else and the vindictive torrent began again.

Finally she sighed and shook her head. The catharsis was over. She relaxed, breathed deeply, and whispered, "That's all. I am cleaned out."

The woman sat down again, calm for a moment. She stretched, reaching her arms overhead and to her sides as far as possible. "I feel good," she whispered, "like a weight has been lifted from my shoulders."

"What you have done is medicine for the spirit," Edward said. "Unloading your mind of the sickening emotions you have been carrying around for years is all part of the healing process. You have let go. And letting go is an absolute requirement for getting well again.

"Come, let's walk," Edward said. "I want to tell you a story about letting go.

"Once, in the town of Old Stonebridge, near the great cliffs, there lived a knight named Morehead. He was revered by all the people of the village for his bravery and devotion to duty. He was in charge of protecting the village from attack by enemies, and he took his work seriously. He commanded the troops with precision and instilled great confidence in all the townspeople.

"One night a band of robbers attacked the village and Morehead was wounded. But because he was brave, he fought on. After the robbers left, the people of the village immediately came to Morehead's aid. They dressed his wound and prepared hot chicken broth for him to eat, hoping for his speedy recovery. And they thanked him for protecting the village.

"But instead of allowing his wound to remain bound and to heal, Morehead took off the bandage whenever any of the townspeople visited him. 'I will show my wound to everyone,' he said.

"And he did. Not only did he remove the dressing, he probed into the wound, examining it and showing it to all who would look. The wound began to fester, became infected, and eventually developed a most unpleasant odor.

"Still Morehead continued to show his wound to anyone who would look, hoping all the people would be grateful for the great sacrifice he had made for their village.

"Before long, the once grateful townspeople no longer cared to visit Morehead, and no one wanted to look at his wound. In fact, the friends who had admired him began to chide him and made unkind remarks behind his back. The knight was left alone with his memories and his pain."

The woman turned to Edward. "What would you have me learn from this story?" she asked.

"I want you to learn about healing wounds, about letting go, and about not always having to be right. And I want you to apply the tonic of forgiveness.

"Morehead's wound was physical, but his preoccupation with it was mental and emotional. He wouldn't allow the wound to heal.

"That is what we do to our emotional wounds when we constantly inspect them, probing for outside causes, fixing blame on others for our hurts. The resentment that results causes our wounds to fester and become infected with the poison of recrimination. We become as unpleasant as the odor from Morehead's wound. Our friends and family begin to withdraw from us until we are alone with our pain, dwelling on our hurts and insults and causing them to infect our minds.

"We have to decide: Do we want to be healed? Or do we want to go on rehearsing our wounds, all the while triggering increasingly negative emotions that cause our well-being to suffer? Always having to be right and then resenting anyone who challenges our positions, or maybe even retaliating against them, causes us to have toxic souls and corrodes the joy that is possible in our lives.

"Yes, we have wounds, but can we, will we, allow our wounds to remain bandaged and healing to take place? Those who rehearse the hurts and frustrations of the past, carrying with them thoughts of resentment and recrimination, assume a terrible affliction that becomes an overwhelming burden, one which may even contribute to their physical demise. That burden is guilt.

"This is where the soothing salve of forgiveness does its quiet miracle. Forgiveness helps us remember with compassion. The cycle of resentment, recrimination, and remorse is ended. We are healed of the haunted past.

"Forgiveness is one of life's most precious treasures and a sure sign of wellness."

Forgiveness, the woman thought, is a very difficult issue. Sometimes I don't really like to forgive. In other cases I don't want to forgive. If a person has committed an overt act, perhaps he or she deserves compassion. But there are some actions that simply are unforgivable.

"How can we possibly forgive some people?" she asked. "Murderers. Rapists. Child molesters. Recently I heard the story of a father who actually set fire to his son. Are you suggesting that even actions of that kind should be forgiven? How can that be possible?"

"Put the focus on who benefits most from the forgiving," Edward said. "We do, the ones who do the forgiving. It's not so much that we let the other person off the hook, but that we let ourselves off the hook and can stop investing all our emotional energy in holding onto perceived wrongs. Our energy can then be directed toward helping heal our entire lives.

THE TRIUMPHANT PATIENT

"Learn to forgive in three distinct areas: Forgive others, forgive yourself, and forgive God.

"Forgiving others releases us from the burden of carrying the poisonous emotions of hate. Learn to see offenders as the needy persons they really are. That doesn't mean we excuse hurtful behavior or become spineless. No. Instead we simply realize that in their imperfection, these people need not be condemned so much as forgiven.

"Allow them to feel their own guilt and to learn from it. Even in all our wisdom, we cannot change others by pointing out the errors of their ways. That is something they must each do for themselves.

"Our responsibility is limited to ourselves. Our greatest impact on the lives of others is in how we live our lives and not in how we tell them to live theirs."

The woman nodded her understanding.

"Then learn to forgive yourself," Edward said. "We, too, are needy. All of us have hurt other people with behavior that doesn't match our potential. And the more decent we are, the more acutely we feel our pain for the hurts we have caused. Forgive yourself for your own faults. And then realize that these faults do not mean you are a bad person, but mean only that you may have done some bad things. And that is something quite different."

"This is the issue of guilt, isn't it?" asked the woman.

"Yes, but more accurately, it is the issue of remorse and shame," Edward responded. "Holding on to remorse and shame is very destructive. We have opportunities to learn and grow from regret, but remorse and shame only tear at us. They are self-hate. They lead us to feel humiliating disgrace for who we are as persons, and they lead to our demise.

"Regret is our sorrow over our actions, not our persons. We may not have lived up to our potential in our behavior, but it does not mean that we are condemned as persons. We must learn to esteem ourselves as persons with great potential for good. We must learn also to forgive our behaviors that haven't lived up to that potential. This is learning to forgive ourselves."

These distinctions were interesting to the woman. She stopped and jotted down a note before Edward continued.

"And finally, in the third area," Edward continued, "we must learn to forgive God."

"Forgive God? Why would I want to or need to forgive God?" the woman asked.

They were strolling near a bed of beautiful, colorful flowers. Edward bent down and picked one.

"God has created many things perfectly," he said, "such as this flower. But sometimes we mortals do not see all of God's creation as perfect.

"When I was first diagnosed, in no way did I feel my illness might be part of God's plan or could in any way be used for good. And I became angry at God for allowing me to become ill. Then came a large measure of self-pity. How could such a tragedy befall me? I felt I deserved better. How could God do this to me? This thinking led to more anger. God is at fault. Life is not fair. God is to blame. It was a vicious and destructive cycle.

"Forgiving God needs to be a priority, not to let God off the hook but to release ourselves from such paralyzing resentment. We may not approve of all of

God's work, but we can learn to accept this world and trust him, even in the face of life-threatening illness. The result will be that our lives are closer to being healed."

"Didn't you ever ask *why?*" responded the woman. "Why does God ever allow illness and disability and terrible things to happen?"

Edward nodded. "It is so easy to blame God when things go wrong," he said. "We believe God created a perfect world as we would define it. We know he is alive and active. It follows naturally that we would think he has caused every single circumstance of our lives, including illness and disability and terrible things, as well as strong bodies, happiness, and successful lives. We tend to think that God blesses us with good health and happiness when we deserve it and punishes us with illness, disability, and terrible things when that is what we deserve.

"That way of thinking puts us in charge of God. We'll do this and that and God will reward us. We'll do thus and so and he'll punish us. That way of thinking strips God of his infinite wisdom and replaces him with our own human very fallible reasoning. That way of thinking allows us to argue with God, for that is what we do when we ask why.

"When we ask why we are really saying, 'How dare you do this to *me!*' We challenge what has happened, hoping that if we get angry enough, God will change. When we question God, we're not looking for answers, we're trying to have an argument with him, to show him his error. Believe me, there is a better way.

"Instead of asking, 'Why did this happen to me,' ask instead, 'Toward what end?'

"Don't see your illness or disability as God's punishment. It isn't! Understand instead that it's something God can use, and remember that he is there, always there, to walk with you, to guide you in the journey, to help you triumph. That is what he wants for each one of us—to live triumphantly. This allows us to examine what we might do to live more positively now, today, in spite of the threat of illness or any number of other problems in our lives.

"Asking 'Toward what end?' gets us to the point of seeing our illnesses as assets, circumstances that, with proper discipline, can be of help to countless other people. And more importantly, our illnesses can be the very events that mark positive turning points in our own lives.

"Only as we drop our fixation with why and concentrate on how this circumstance can best be used— toward what end?—will we reach our highest potentials."

Edward is right, the woman thought. When she lamented, "Why me," she wasn't looking for answers. She didn't want to know why. She wanted pity, or she was lashing out at life, angry that it had dealt her this cruel blow. Edward's insight was truly revealing.

"Some of the why question is natural," Edward continued. "But observe the people who are stuck on it, who simply cannot move beyond it. They're mired in self-pity. They're the ones who are hateful, full of toxic hostility toward themselves and others."

"And God?" asked the woman.

Edward nodded his agreement. He liked that question. Was the woman beginning to understand?

"Yes," he said, "and this is the very core of the issue

we talked about earlier: *Hate is death. Forgiveness is life.*

"When you forgive, you most surely change yourself. That is the great gift of forgiving. Perhaps more than anything else, this changes the manner in which you perceive yourself and the way others respond to you. And forgiving God will certainly change your perception of the world you live in and the circumstances in which you find yourself.

"Forgiveness is love's toughest work, but it brings love's highest rewards. If we can just bring ourselves to acknowledge a grudge or a prejudice or a bitterness or a blame—toward God, toward others, toward ourselves, or toward the world in general—then we can apply our new and exciting perspective on life: Even if we are the hurt ones, we are seldom the completely innocent ones.

"Once we acknowledge we may have had a part in the problem, we then have something concrete to work with. We can't really change the other person. We can only change ourselves. And the central change that needs to take place is a realization that others are not totally evil and that we are not totally perfect. Then we can understand the issues in terms of forgiveness. We can accept the situation, we can accept our part in it, and we can take responsibility for resolving it.

"A large part of your wellness journey truly distills into this: Forgive yourself for the wrongs you've done to others, both acts of commission and omission. Then forgive, even bless, those who have wronged you. Wish each one well in your mind and heart and release them to their highest good. Then forgive God. As you do, you will break the chains of shame and remorse that have imprisoned you.

"Make forgiveness a habit. When the Master was asked how often we should forgive, he answered, 'seventy times seven.' He was telling us to forgive infinitely. If one is seeking a triumphant life," Edward concluded, "this is the most important lesson."

Once again the triumphant journey brought the woman face to face with herself. She realized that one certainly spends a great deal of time looking within. And the issue of forgiveness was a difficult one. She knew it was something with which she needed to deal, and that it was not pleasant.

"I feel you are telling me to perform mental and spiritual self-surgery," she said.

"Well put," Edward said as he smiled. "But I detect sorrow and hesitation in your voice. Just allow me to reassure you that forgiveness puts our spirits in order. Then healing comes.

"That is why it is so important to comprehend that *hate is death; forgiveness is life*. It is a fact to be honored not a warning to fear."

The woman was thoughtful. "You know," she said, "just venting the feelings I had pent up has made me feel better. I sense forgiveness can help me continue to feel even better."

"Forgiveness helped me achieve personal peace," Edward said. "When I didn't have to always be right, when I could forgive myself and others, I began to know a serenity unlike anything I had ever known before. It has resulted in a continuing sense of well-being. And I believe it has added to my wellness and recovery. It will do the same for you."

"What should I do?" the woman asked quietly.

Edward smiled. Was this the quiet breakthrough

he'd hoped for? It was a tender moment. They sat together on a nearby bench.

"Each person must find his own way," he said. "But I can share with you my experience and ask if it is something you too would like to do.

"The first thing I did was write a list of all the people with whom I had emotional conflicts that needed to be resolved. I started the list with myself, and I added everyone I could think of.

"Then I went down the list name by name, saying out loud an affirmation of forgiveness toward each person.

"One person was named Beatrice. Out loud I said, 'Beatrice, I totally forgive you.' And I said it again. I even said it a third time emphatically and with volume, 'Beatrice, I totally and completely forgive you.'"

Edward smiled. The woman chuckled. "You say that with such force," she said.

"I said it and I meant it. I was convinced that only bad things would come to me if I continued to hate. I spoke so forcefully because I wanted this resolved so much. And I hope you will do it the same way.

"Go down the list of each person you told me about. One at a time out loud say their names and 'I totally and completely forgive you.'

"Next I actually imagined good things happening to each of these people," continued Edward. "In fact, I prayed for each of my former enemies. I quietly imagined them happy and content in their lives. Then I prayed, 'Dear God, be with my friend Beatrice. And renew in me the ability to love her without judging her. Amen.'

"I did this with each person I needed to forgive. I

spent nearly two hours one day in this exercise. It was a wonderful experience," Edward said. "Perhaps you will want to try it too."

"I don't know," pondered the woman. "Pray for them? See good things happening to them? Is this what is really required to forgive?"

"For me it was," Edward said. "The Triumphant Patient teaches this as a formula for forgiveness. It has worked for thousands of people. I think it could work for you as well, if you'll try it."

The woman was thoughtful. This was such revolutionary thinking for her. The process of forgiving seemed risky. She thought she would be vulnerable.

"Is there more?" she asked.

"Yes," Edward said. "There may be some cases where amends need to be made. I had to do this with a co-worker named Wilfred. We'd had a bitter falling out over an issue, and neither of us could admit wrong. We kept a serious feud going.

"Then I became ill. And, this is the absolute truth, within thirty days Wilfred also became ill. Of course I cannot prove that our illnesses were caused by our ongoing feud, but I do know this war consumed both of us at times. I am certain it contributed to my illness.

"I became convinced that my lack of forgiveness was preventing my recovery, and I summoned every ounce of courage I possessed, gave Wilfred a call, and asked if I could come by to talk to him.

"It was the most difficult thing I have ever done. I was shaking as I approached his door. My heart was pounding. I was nervous and even afraid.

"We talked. I found the ability, in a stumbling, faltering way, to say I was truly sorry for the wrong I had caused him and for the ill feelings I held toward him. I said I wanted to heal the situation and to be on the best terms we could salvage from the experience."

"What was his response?" asked the woman.

"He replied that he was the one who needed to ask forgiveness," Edward said. "And he did. Then we stood and hugged and cried, two grown men expressing sincere regret. It touches me now just to think of it."

The woman had tears in her eyes. She too was touched.

"I came away from Wilfred's home a free person. It was like 'Whew!' A load was taken off my shoulders. Once I made amends in this way, I had a clean conscience."

"I have a similar situation," said the woman, "but I don't think I could possibly face that person. Do you think I really need to go see her?"

"Only if you want to enhance your health and enrich your life," Edward said.

There was a long pause. Of course that was what she wanted, but what Edward had talked about took courage. And her pride would have to take a back seat. But it must be done. It was not too high a price for abundant life.

"Okay, I'll try," she said. "It frightens me, but I'll do it."

"Wonderful," Edward said.

"Then do one final thing. Forgive God and ask God to forgive you. Ask God to improve you in any way that needs improving."

"Oh, I don't know," responded the woman. "I'm just not a religious person. I don't go to church, and I doubt God would be interested in hearing my prayers."

"Perhaps that is a subject for another day," Edward replied. "But I want you to know that when I was able to forgive God for whatever I thought wasn't right, I received a tremendous knowledge of forgiveness in return. This is another of the great gifts of forgiveness, and it works two ways. When you forgive, you are forgiven."

The woman nodded her understanding.

"This week make forgiveness your primary focus," Edward said. "And at the end of the week, evaluate your journey. I believe it will make a huge difference in your life. Remember, forgiveness is life—your life."

The woman smiled, knowing full well the challenge she had been given.

As they left each other, she made some notes so she could remember the meeting.

Forgiveness

- Forgiveness frees me to heal my entire life.
- I do not always have to be right.
- Forgiveness puts my spirit in order. Then healing can come.
- Hate is my death. Forgiveness means life.
- To forgive:—Make a list of those I need to forgive. Start with myself.
  —Say out loud, "_____, I totally forgive you."
  —Pray for and imagine good things happening to that person.
  —Make amends as required.
  —Forgive God. Ask God to forgive me.

Chapter 6

THE CALL
TO LOVE

T he woman's next assignment was to meet with Britta, and she prepared for their visit with great anticipation. Britta, somewhat of a local celebrity, was quite an extraordinary person. She owned and operated Britta's Place, a well-known and very popular restaurant, and she was known as a culinary expert. She was often invited to appear on local television programs to demonstrate table settings, cooking techniques, and the methods involved in preparing some of her more famous recipes.

But the quality that drew people to Britta's Place, perhaps more so than the delicious food and excellent service, was Britta herself. She was usually at the door to warmly greet her guests. She would ask their names and see that they were seated comfortably and served quickly with charm and elegance by her efficient staff. She was at the door to say goodbye when they left, calling each by name and inviting them to come again soon. And she rarely forgot a name.

When Britta's Place patrons left the restaurant they took with them the warm feeling that Britta and her staff really cared about them. They wanted to return again and again. And they did. In fact, so many returned so often, it wasn't unusual to have to wait thirty minutes or more for a table. But they didn't mind. Britta made the waiting pleasant. They watched her whisk from table to table, in and out of the kitchen, greeting, chatting, saying goodbye, running her business with charm, grace, and efficiency.

And Britta did all of this from her bright purple wheelchair.

The woman was to meet Britta at the restaurant for a late lunch after the noon hour rush had subsided. But she was so anxious to learn the next step she would take on her triumphant journey, she couldn't wait. She wanted to be nearby Britta's Place as early as possible. Perhaps some of the next principle of wellness would be apparent to her just by being close to Britta.

She decided to spend some time walking along the shore of the lake near the restaurant. The wind off the water was brisk and invigorating. As she strolled alone along the shore, she had time to think about her journey.

The woman was encouraged. The first thing she realized was that she was comfortable for the first time in her life being alone. She'd always thought being alone was the same as being lonely, and she'd often been lonely, even when she was around other people. But she'd learned the difference, and she knew she was comfortable alone because she'd grown to like herself. Once she'd chosen to be hopeful, to change her mind and focus on positive beliefs, and to meditate to calm her mind and let go of her negative emotions, she'd discovered that she had many good qualities that she liked. Then when she had begun to work on forgiving, she'd had another breakthrough.

She'd made a list the way Edward suggested and actually wrote on paper the names of people with whom she'd had conflict. She wrote five names. Then she wrote her own name at the top as Edward said she should, but when she began to affirm those on the list, she began with the second name. She whispered the name and said softly, "I totally and completely forgive you." She closed her eyes and tried to imagine that person having all the good and wonderful things he wanted. Then she prayed the prayer Edward had taught her, "Dear God, be with my friend and renew in me the ability to love him without judging him. Amen."

She affirmed all the people on the list, except the first one—herself. Then she waited. She felt no different, and she thought she should. She went through the list again, whispering the five names, saying "I totally and completely forgive you," and praying the short prayer. She did this three times.

Then she remembered some others, added those names, and went through the list again several times. She began to call out the names, louder each time, until she was almost exhausted.

She closed her eyes and began to meditate: breathe in, breathe out, *peace*, but her mind would not cooperate. Thoughts flooded in. She couldn't dismiss them, couldn't let them go. Gradually they became one thought: *Forgiving others is the easy part. You must forgive yourself.*

But she didn't know how.

She closed her eyes and prayed, "Dear God, be with *me* and renew in me the ability to love myself. Help me to forgive myself. And, dear God, please forgive me. Amen."

A new sense of serenity came to her, a peacefulness like she'd never known before. She felt safe, esteemed, whole. A new thought began to form in her mind: *You don't have to be perfect to know love or to give love. You can't undo the past, but you can make amends. And you can begin today to make a difference in the lives of others through love and compassion, understanding and joy. Your life can be joyful no matter how long you live, no matter what your circumstances. You have great potential.*

The anger was gone and in its place was a sense of well-being. Since that day she had made a conscious effort to reframe the people and circumstances of her life as opportunities to learn. And when she did, she discovered a gift in every one of these situations.

Forgiveness gave her freedom. She was no longer condemned to a prison of judgment and inadequacy. She felt she was learning and growing as a person from these encounters. It was a new and exciting discovery, and she began to sense the potential power in her life of forgiveness.

It hadn't all been smooth sailing though. One evening a thought overwhelmed her: "Does forgiving mean that I am giving permission to these people to repeat their behavior?"

That question had been troublesome, for clearly she did not care to have the same experiences with some of the people on her list.

But she was becoming wise. She understood that the two were not connected. The same experiences would happen again only if she allowed them; she'd have to give permission for such events to take place.

With the tool of forgiveness and a keener insight into all she could do to help in her own healing, she came to realize that her situation was far from desperate. She had much to say about its course.

At midweek she had a favorable visit with her doctors. It was not all positive—there were still problems—but everyone was pleased with progress in several areas. And some had commented that her spirits were better. Not only did she feel better, others could tell she did.

She walked quickly toward Britta's Place. Finally it was time. She could see Britta at the door.

Britta greeted the woman warmly and led her to a table in a corner.

As they were being seated, the woman reflected briefly on the many different types of people she had met on her triumphant patient journey. Young, old, male, female, all from different ethnic backgrounds. Some were plain-spoken. Others, like Britta, seemed sophisticated. It was interesting to observe that seemingly anyone was able to become triumphant.

Like the others, Britta had an underlying quality of serenity. The woman wondered which came first, serenity or wellness. Soon she would ask.

"My triumphant friends have been telling me about you," Britta said, smiling. "And they say you are doing well. How would you judge your progress?"

"I'm feeling better about myself than I have in years," replied the woman. "I'm truly hopeful. I've substituted more helpful beliefs and I'm using my mind positively in the healing process. And the whole discipline of forgiveness has freed me from years of emotional imprisonment. That has given me pure joy!

"But I sense I have a long way to go. My life is still filled with uncertainty. I want to be well. And that desire stands in the way of any real and lasting happiness."

Britta reflected a moment before responding, yet her eyes never left the woman's. Britta's silence was part of her answer. Quietly she began.

"It need not stand in your way, you know," she said.

"Yes, but it's my illness and all the unknowns that are so unsettling," replied the woman.

Once again Britta's reply was quiet and filled with compassion. "I want you to know one thing clearly as a result of our meeting today. You can choose to be well now, no matter what the state of your illness, no matter how many unknowns you have in your life."

The woman challenged Britta. "I wouldn't be unhappy if I could help it. I want to be well."

"That's the point," said Britta. "You can indeed help it. Wellness doesn't just happen by accident. It is something that we consciously choose.

"Now I didn't say we can choose to be cured. I said we can choose to be *well*. But the two are inextricably linked."

"I don't get it," the woman said. "If my situation were different, if I owned a restaurant, if my illness was cured, then perhaps I could believe what you say. But not now, not at this time."

Britta smiled. Her triumphant friends had told her the woman was full of potential. But they also had warned she was surprisingly resistant.

Lovingly Britta continued. "Today I want you to challenge that belief," she said. "I encourage you to rise to a new level of understanding, to learn the difference between acceptance and approval. If you will carefully consider the issue of love in your life and its awesome power for wellness, it will change your life.

"Let me share the story of two friends. Clare and Lacey both live in this city. Each is married and each happens to have three children. They share the same faith.

"Clare has kidney disease and her life is limited by her need for dialysis and all the different protocols that go with her condition. Lacey has diabetes but is able to live quite normally with attention to diet and the help of insulin.

"Clare bubbles with enthusiasm. She is happy to be alive and isn't afraid to show it. She is a joy to be with and you always get a lift from just being around her.

"Lacey is best described as dour. Something is almost always wrong or about to be wrong. For her, life has to be endured.

"I'm fascinated by the contrast between these two women," Britta continued. "Clare, who has continuing difficulties with her illness, comes from a family with very limited means. They live in a modest section of town, drive a car that is constantly in need of repair, and have what many people would call a difficult life. She waits tables for us part-time to earn extra money. Still, Clare is full of joy.

"Lacey, whose physical condition has been stable for some time, is a person of no small means. Her husband owns his own business and is quite successful. Her home is in the finest section of town overlooking the water. They always seem to have new prestigious cars and the family travels extensively and often entertains lavishly. In fact, they recently had our staff cater an expensive private party. But Lacey is joyless.

"Now, who do you think should be the happy one?" Britta asked.

The woman smiled. The point was obvious. She looked at Britta and shrugged her shoulders. "Lacey, of course," she answered.

"But Lacey isn't happy," Britta said. "How can it be that life is so much more wonderful for Clare than for Lacey?

"I believe the key is this: Their happiness has nothing to do with the actual circumstances of their lives or the state of their health, but it has everything to do with the kind of love in their lives.

"Lacey operates from conditional love. She has to have everything in life meet her approval. Clare lives her life from unconditional love. She has learned the power of acceptance. And this simple decision has massive life-changing implications."

"Conditional? Unconditional? Acceptance? Approval? What do you mean?" asked the woman.

Britta responded, "Quite simply, if you can learn to accept without having to approve, you are practicing unconditional love. The practice of unconditional love will change your entire experience of illness and life."

"That's a pretty strong statement," said the woman.

"Yes, it is," Britta replied. "And still it is an understatement, for love is who and what you truly are.

"We all want wellness—mental, emotional, spiritual, and especially physical wellness. We want to live long lives. We all believe we want less stress, less depression, less resentment.

"But because we get so confused as to who we really are, we become preoccupied with the physical, with our bodies. And when we do, we miss the essence of who we truly are—spirits with the potential for love."

The woman looked perplexed. "I don't understand," she said. "You're not making any sense to me."

"Okay," Britta said. "Consider for a moment who you really are. On one level you are a physical reality. You are your body and all its needs. You are also your emotions, your subconscious drives, your ego. On another level, you are your mind, a mental being with rational thoughts and capabilities. All these are you. And all are important.

"But there is an even higher you, the spiritual you. With our spiritual selves we reach for our ultimate potential as human beings. It is there that we meet the real and lasting eternal self.

"The trouble is that we spend most of our lives functioning on our lower levels. Most of our lives are lived caring for our bodies and fulfilling or defending our emotions. And when we are ill or disabled, we often become obsessed with the physical and are controlled by our negative emotions. But that is not who we really are."

The woman sensed she was listening to something of great importance to her. But she simply didn't grasp the dimensions of what Britta was saying.

"What would you have me do?" she asked.

Britta continued. "I would have you look within," she said. "And I would have you see wellness on the spiritual level as your primary goal. To reach that goal, the practice of unconditional love will be your new aim.

"You see, most of our conscious lives are spent on the physical level. And most of the time we do not choose the spiritual quality of peace over conflict because we fear. We carry strange beliefs, such as revenge will give us satisfaction or we will look better if we can prove someone else wrong."

The woman nodded her understanding. "I've come to understand that these past few days in my forgiveness work."

"And sometimes," Britta continued, "we try to blame others or circumstances for our plight."

The woman smiled an uneasy grin. "That describes me too."

"Or maybe we attempt to manipulate another by guilt," Britta said. "Some people even resort to force or violence. And we tend to believe people deserve the pain they receive.

"But then we are at a loss to explain why this competitive I-must-win-you-must-lose approach to life does not yield wellness and peace. We become preoccupied with life on the lowest levels. Body, emotions, the mind consume us. There is no room for the spirit."

This the woman understood, and she nodded in agreement.

"When illness or disability strike," Britta continued, "in a real sense we become captives of the physical, powerless over body, emotions, and mind. We think we've been betrayed by all that we have based our lives on."

"Oh yes," said the woman. "I do understand. You are describing me."

"I am describing all of us who have faced life-threatening or life-impairing disabilities," Britta said.

"We each feel betrayed by a body gone awry, become trapped by emotions that are filled with fear, and pounded by a mind that can only 'awfulize' and predict doom.

"What we need is an experience that will raise our level of awareness to our highest level—the spiritual. This certainly heals. In fact true healing, complete healing, has at its roots the ability to give and receive unconditional love.

"This experience begins by first identifying less with our bodies," Britta continued. "Our perception of who we are shifts from our bodies and emotions through our minds to our spirits. And there we recognize our true identities—love."

"But our bodies are the central parts of our lives," objected the woman. "To deny that reality is wrong."

"I'm not suggesting that you deny the reality of your body. I want you to take that reality into a new dimension. The Triumphant Patient helps us see that our task is to develop an outlook that puts our bodies into perspective, that our bodies are servants to our spirits.

"When we are ill, we tend to downplay, or even ignore altogether, our greatest asset, our spiritual essence."

"I have a sense you are asking me to make vast changes in my life," the woman said.

"I'm asking you to change within," Britta replied. "I am asking you to change your perspective of life. I am asking you to consider that you are first a spiritual reality that is having a physical experience. If you can reach this level of conscious awareness, you will change your entire life—body, emotions, mind, and spirit."

Although the woman didn't speak, Britta could sense she was skeptical and unsure.

"Many people get frightened by this step of the triumphant journey," Britta continued. "Their perception is that their daily lives will be filled with deprivation and discontent. But nothing is farther from the truth. What we seek is an inner awareness of our true natures, our spiritual natures.

"Once we recognize our spiritual natures, any external changes, if they are required, will occur naturally. There'll be no deprivation. There will come an enrichment from knowing who we are."

The woman stopped Britta. "I don't follow," she said. "I thought illness was a message to change. But this is, well, it's weird."

Britta was patient with the woman. She understood, for she too had made this journey.

"In a sense it is weird, for it is not what one would rationally predict. The twist is this: Change on the spiritual level is concerned not so much with what we do with our lives as it is with how we do it.

"Are we living our lives with love even though we may be experiencing illness or disability? Do we conduct ourselves with peace and serenity? This is the nature of the spiritual, and change is concerned with the *how*. The *what* will follow."

The woman interjected, "But we don't really live our lives here, on this spiritual level. That is something for monks or saints, not everyday living."

"Oh, this is truly for everyday living," Britta said. "And while we may not have lived our lives here, I am asking you to let illness redirect you and set you on a more spiritual path, for this is where you'll find your wellness."

Skepticism showed on the woman's face and in her posture. Yet Britta continued calmly.

"Unconditional love is what we are after. It is the part of us that is real, the part that is eternal. This love cannot be imprisoned by the merely physical, by a body we may have judged to have gone haywire. This love transcends and even affects the physical. And this love will change the way we experience our lives, no matter what our circumstances."

"Frankly, I think I am not interested in this," the woman said. "I want to be well. I want to get my life back to normal again. Look at you in that wheelchair. Don't you think your body betrayed you? I know mine did me. I want that changed!"

"I used to believe my body had betrayed me," Britta said. "But for the past decade or longer, I have believed my accident was a gift!"

"A gift?" the woman responded, pulling back and wrinkling her brow. "What are you saying? It completely changed your life."

Britta nodded. "It certainly did. And all for good. I don't want to confront you, but why do you assume that your illness or my disability is negative?"

"How can it be anything but negative?" the woman responded.

"On the spiritual path, your illness and my disability can indeed be turning points, something to be respected and honored. Illness or disability can redirect your life if you will let it."

"I still don't see it," said the woman.

"When I say my disability was a gift, I mean it was an invitation for me to change my life. In fact, I'm not certain I could have this wonderful life today had it not been for the accident. It taught me to love without condition.

"How can I fully explain this to you?" Britta asked. "Each must experience it personally. When I made the decision to walk the spiritual path and see love as my primary aim, my disability no longer had any power over me. In a real sense, I was healed.

"Mai is a friend who has lupus. She stopped trying to effect a physical cure through her considerable personal efforts and turned her medical care over to a team she trusted. She continued to participate in decision-making and was still involved with her care. But her physical condition was no longer her primary focus. Then she was able to move to the spiritual level. And that is where love did its work. Instead of living with struggle and strife, today Mai is leading a life that is full and vibrant, even though she has physical limitations.

"The difference? Unconditional love is her new goal. Her wellness follows."

The woman was quiet. Britta offered another example.

"Vivian has rheumatoid arthritis. For years her real struggle and anguish came from trying to control something that she couldn't completely control, her physical degeneration. But then she had the good fortune to meet the Triumphant Patient. With the encouragement of many people, Vivian gave up her attachment to her struggles and chose to pursue love.

"She no longer judges her success by the state of her illness. Instead, now she is committed to judging her life's success by the love she was able to give. She chose to identify not with her body, but with her spirit. To this day she is pain free and her health and total well-being remain at the highest point in nearly twenty-two years."

Britta looked directly at the woman. "Why?" she asked. "Such is the power of love. I know her success is due in part to her choice of spirit over body."

The woman listened to these stories with deep respect. Still she had doubts.

"But how can I make this real in my own life?" she asked. "I'm concerned that this sort of thing happens only to a fortunate few. What guarantees do I have for my life?"

"You do have guarantees," Britta assured. "The guarantees are that you will have a better life no matter what the length. You will touch lives more deeply than you ever have before. You will know peace, a true spiritual serenity, like you've never known before. That is wellness on the highest level!"

Britta grasped the woman's arm. "It is the pain in our lives, the emotional upheaval, that causes us to change. Isn't it time to let go of that pain, to drop the angst over your physical wellness?

"If you can let go of the anguish and allow unconditional love to govern your life, every day will be a blessing. You will know that all that is happening to you is not a tragedy. And you will become a channel for love in the service of others. There is no higher call."

Once again the woman was thoughtful, not knowing how to react to all she had heard. Finally she asked, "But what do I get out of it?"

Britta realized by this question that the woman had not accepted all she'd said. What could she do? What could she say? This was one of the most important steps in the triumphant patient's journey. Those who resisted never seemed to find peace.

"What you get is life, more abundant life. You get

yourself beyond seeing life and relationships as transactions when you think in terms of getting. When you think only of getting, all the getting will never fill that vague void within. Such voids are only filled by love.

"You'll discover the special gift of your illness. This is that spiritual opportunity to come to see yourself as a whole person, one who is complete and has the potential for greatness. You will be able to love yourself, to see yourself from a position of strength, spiritual strength.

"And you'll come to know a new peace in life, God's peace. That's a precious and priceless gift that will change your life.

"I know this seems difficult, even unbelievable to you," Britta said. "But I ask you to release your focus on the physical. Give up your judgment that this affliction is bad. Instead allow your mind to rest on the spirit of unconditional love. See this as an extension of the work of forgiveness.

"When you do, your life will be transformed, and your wellness assured."

The woman knew she had work to do. It would be difficult to change her perspective as Britta was suggesting, for she still wanted a cure if that could be possible.

Finally she responded. "Can love heal?" she asked.

"Oh, indeed. And I believe it may also help cure. Love is an immense *live* message through our spirits to our bodies. But believe me, that will become secondary, for the practice of unconditional love will reshape you into its likeness. You will become well as you become one with love. And to that wellness, there is no end.

"When we can allow our spirits to forget the need to judge, we have traveled a long, long way toward releasing ourselves from the prison of approval. We can accept without having to approve."

"But that means resignation. To me it is giving up," countered the woman.

"No," replied Britta. "When we accept, we get closer to loving without condition. We can love without expecting anything in return. And when we do so, we release tremendous energy for healing. In that sense unconditional love is a powerful stimulant to our healing process.

"Love becomes more than emotion. Love becomes physiological reality. In a real sense, love creates wellness. And it may also cure illness.

"That's why the Triumphant Patient defines wellness as 'the attainment of personal peace, knowing God's peace.' And healing is described as 'releasing our fears, fears that cause us to love with conditions.'

"This is very important," Britta said, "and I believe it is most profound. When we can love without any condition, we indeed know peace. Freeing ourselves from fears, angers, and guilt allows us to live fully this moment, no matter what the circumstances. You see, that peace is totally independent from physical condition.

"That, dear friend, is what attaining the status of 'triumphant' is all about."

Britta was quiet. The woman was thoughtful. For the first time she understood where those who are triumphant find their serenity. So this is how forgiveness and unconditional love work together. It was a whole new perspective for the woman, and it required that she give up so many previous beliefs.

"So, are inner peace and serenity the goal?" asked the woman.

"Yes," replied Britta. "The goal is knowing God's peace."

"But what happened to my healing?"

"We look at healing as a side benefit to the attainment of personal peace," responded Britta. "Personal peace, knowing God's peace, living in God's joy, each and every day, *that* is the goal. I can only tell you that for thousands of people this has also resulted in physical healing.

"Some people say that the search for a physical cure is their most important consideration. But not those on the triumphant path. No. For us, it is knowing God's peace. That comes from forgiveness and unconditional love. The physical healing is a welcome by-product, but it is never a requirement for a complete and fulfilling life.

"Understand that this is what you are called to do and to be. This is your life's goal, your reason for living. You are called to a life of giving and receiving unconditional love. You are called to be a conduit for God's love no matter what your physical circumstances.

"Oh, if you could truly understand and act on this, you would be the 'wellest' person in the world." Britta sighed wistfully. "This is my greatest pursuit."

"Do you ever attain this perfect unconditional love?" asked the woman.

"For me it is a continuing part of the triumphant journey," said Britta. "It is not a matter of arriving at a certain stage and then the accomplishment is complete.

"This is an ongoing journey. It is a new way of living. And as long as our bodies are alive, our task is to use them as a means of extending unconditional love to others. It changes not only your experience of illness, but your experience of life. In a real sense, unconditional love heals your whole life. And this healing is just a choice away."

The woman was again quiet and thoughtful. Finally Britta gently touched the woman's arm and spoke softly. "Go now. Let your aim be unconditional love and see the difference it makes in your life. Do this now."

The woman thanked Britta. Then she went back near the water, found a quiet place, and made these notes.

The Call to Love

—When I learn to accept without having to approve, I am practicing unconditional love.

—Love is my true nature, my highest spiritual self.

—Healing has at its roots the ability to give and receive unconditional love.

—Love cannot be limited by the merely physical.

—The goal is to know personal peace. This comes from understanding that my purpose is to be a conduit for God's love.

—The ability to know personal peace is independent from my physical condition.

—Unconditional love heals my whole life.

Chapter 7

Transformed for Living

"The *real you* is your spirit. That is what will live forever," he said.

The woman and the Triumphant Patient were again sitting together on the deck at the rear of his house. After visiting with all the friends he had suggested she meet, she had returned to him to talk about why the triumphant path works and to further discuss the benefits of becoming a triumphant patient.

"Your spirit is not confined to your body," he said. "Life and the body simply are not the same. And the implications of this are enormous."

"Look," said the woman. "I am not a religious person. I've been to church only a few times in my adult life and I simply am not comfortable talking about religion. I would like to talk about unconditional love, the subject Britta discussed with me. I haven't gotten a good focus on that. Would you mind if we move on to that?"

"I understand what you are saying," he responded, "and I share your feeling. I don't consider myself a religious person either, but I do make an effort to be spiritual. There is a vast difference."

"There is?"

"Oh, yes," he said. "Being 'religious' is adhering to doctrines and creeds. But spirituality involves the issues of unconditional love, forgiveness, and following God's will, often something quite different from practicing religion.

"The journey you have begun is a spiritual one. The people you have talked with have actually been helping you create a map for your personal spiritual growth. They have been trying to help you understand how you can take the darkest hour of your life and make it a turning point, to help you move toward your highest good."

"Are you saying that religious people aren't spiritual?"

"From my experience, many aren't. In fact, some of the most religious people I have met are some of the least spiritual."

"Really?" questioned the woman. "I am surprised."

The Triumphant Patient nodded.

"I was surprised also," he said. "And I don't say this in judgment. I'm simply reporting the facts.

"Many of those who would hold themselves up as examples of religious truth are very judgmental. And forgiveness—well, that's something that is often easier to preach than to practice."

The woman had already learned that forgiveness is

easier to talk about than to do. She could easily agree with the Triumphant Patient about that. But she'd always thought going to church was being spiritual. Even though the few times she'd been to church she didn't sense much spirituality, she'd thought that was because it just wasn't for her.

Now that she thought about it, though, what she'd missed in church was a sense of God's presence. The experience didn't touch her. It made her uncomfortable instead. She began to wonder if perhaps it was some of the people associated with religion that made her uncomfortable rather than religion itself.

Since the day she'd prayed for God's help in forgiving herself and asked God to forgive her, she'd become aware of some kind of presence when she prayed. And surprisingly she'd begun to pray more often. Over time the feeling of a presence had intensified. She'd felt almost like she was talking to someone—someone who had great understanding and compassion. Was that God?

"Learn to become aware of the difference between religion and spirituality," the Triumphant Patient said. "Spirituality, particularly unconditional love, forgiveness, and following God's will, is the key to knowing and living God's peace in your life. And that may or may not be found in many religions."

The Triumphant Patient wanted so much for the woman to be open to this great hope. Afraid he would alienate her, he proceeded gently.

"Would you allow me a personal story?" he asked.

The woman nodded her assent.

"Near my childhood home," he said, "there was a very large tree. It was just across the street from our house, and it was a mighty specimen, with wide branches of lush, dark green foliage. It towered over the other trees.

"One night a fierce storm swept through the area. It was an awesome storm. Powerful torrents of rain slashed against our house, and the wind was mighty and strong. The windows shook and rattled and the house quivered from the wind's force. The sky was filled with brilliant flashes of lightning, and cracks of thunder roared like angry cannons. This storm caused serious damage for miles around.

"The electricity went out, and our house was plunged into darkness. We were all frightened, especially the children. Someone found a flashlight and a battery-operated radio, and we huddled near the front door.

"Through the door's window, we could see the towering tree being whipped by the storm. Silhouetted by flashes of lightning against the black sky, its seemingly immovable branches were being tossed like a teeter-totter, first up, then back down. The leaves were sucked off the branches as though they were caught in the draft of a jet engine. It seemed the entire tree would be jerked from the ground and thrown crashing into the street.

"On and on for nearly an hour the storm raged, savagely attacking the tree. But it stood. There was some damage, but the tree survived.

"The next day we children went to inspect. We saw that two huge limbs had snapped, and most of the leaves were gone. But the tree was still there. With some pruning, it survived and thrived.

"Do you know why?" he asked.

The woman smiled. She wondered what point the Triumphant Patient would make with his story.

"The tree withstood the storm not because of its many leaves, not because of its huge branches, and not because of its large round trunk. Certainly they were part of its strength, but there was something else, something more basic that made survival possible.

"That tree survived because of its roots."

The woman chuckled. "Its roots?" she asked.

"Yes. Its roots," he repeated. "Later I learned that type of tree develops a root system nearly equal to the size of its branches and leaves. That tree's root system matched its mass. And the root system, deep and strong, was the reason the tree survived."

"That's interesting," the woman said, "but what are you trying to tell me?"

"You are being buffeted by a fierce storm with this illness," he said. "You're being tossed by the wind. The rain is driving against you. The danger is fierce and at times destruction seems certain. Now, as never before, is the time to draw on the strength of your spiritual roots. And my fear is that those roots may not be deep enough.

"Deepening your spiritual roots, strengthening them with unconditional love and forgiveness and focusing on following God's will—that is the destination of the triumphant patient's journey. It is the only way to truly triumph over illness and to experience life."

"I'm willing to do whatever I need to do," the woman said. "I want to be well. I want to be cured! I want my life to get back to normal—the way it was before my body was invaded by illness.

"I've listened to you and Maria and Susan and Edward and Britta and all the others. I've tried to do what all of you told me, even though I was hesitant at first. I've learned a great deal, and all of it has helped me. I've learned to be hopeful. I've learned to be positive and focus my beliefs on wellness. I've learned to calm my mind and let go of my negative thoughts. I've learned to live just today. I've taken charge of my illness and participated in decisions about my treatment. I've even imagined the treatments and medicines working to rid my body of all signs of my illness. I've forgiven. I've made amends where I needed to.

"I did all of it because I want to be well. And I'm still not! Yet that's what I want and I want it now, today!

"I want to be the way I was," she said, and she began to weep.

The Triumphant Patient waited. Finally he responded.

"Are you sure?" he asked in his quiet, kind voice. "The way you were—is that what you really want?"

"Of course it is," the woman whispered. "I want to be cured."

"Just for a moment," he said, "think deeper and look longer.

"Do you really want your life to be again what it once was? I remember you telling me how difficult it was, how tormented you were. Is it possible that you have really been searching for a better life, no matter what the length?"

She considered his questions. Did she really want her old life again?

No, she didn't want to live again the way she'd lived before. She had tasted unconditional love and forgiveness, and that had given her a new sense of . . . what? How would she describe it? Joy? Peace? Yes, that and more.

"No," she said hesitantly. "I really don't want my old life again. But I don't want my life to end either. There have been times when I wanted to die, to get it over with. Then, almost immediately, I wanted to live. That is when I would be angry again. And honestly, I still feel angry about my illness. I don't know why it has happened to me, why God has made it happen.

"All I've ever known God to do is to judge and punish, and he seems to have punished me more than my share. Maybe that's why I'm ill?"

The Triumphant Patient felt discouraged. He recognized in her words an inaccurate understanding of God and that misperception probably was blocking the woman's wellness. She thought of herself as someone who could do only wrong and of God as only punishing wrongdoing. If she was to have any hope of knowing God's peace, she would need to change her concept of God to have balance in her understanding of his control of her life.

The Triumphant Patient began carefully.

"I made a discovery several years ago that shocked me," he said. "In fact, to this day I marvel at it."

He paused, giving the woman a chance to give her attention to him.

"God does not condemn people who do wrong!" he said.

"That's not true!" the woman responded, throwing out a challenge.

"Oh, but it is," the Triumphant Patient said with

great feeling. "It is not only true, it is a monumental truth that we let slip from our understanding.

"God does not condemn people who do wrong!" he repeated.

"*People*. Put the emphasis on *people*. God does not condemn the person. He disapproves of some behavior, and that's quite different."

The woman was thoughtful, eager to understand this distinction.

"There is, I believe, only one person whom God denounces as a person—the imposter, the person who excuses his or her own wrongdoing while condemning that of another.

"It's interesting. Of all the things God might judge, he chooses to condemn the pretense of virtue, what we call self-righteousness, as the number one issue."

"I'm not certain I understand the point you are making," the woman said.

"God is not simply a mean old judge," he said.

"In fact, it seems to me that the only person God actually judges is the one who cannot perceive the flaws within his or her own heart. God cannot give the gifts of joy and peace to someone who is always critical of others."

Some of the pieces began to fall in place as the woman thought of her experience with forgiveness and unconditional love.

"Tell me more," she said.

"Whenever we criticize or judge or label, we do so to our own detriment. The judgmental person reflects himself in his judgment. He criticizes and condemns someone else, but he is actually projecting himself, his own critical, condemning self. When we label someone, we do not define that person. When we label another, we actually define ourselves.

"That is the antithesis of the direction in which you want to be moving your life. You want to move in the direction of personal spiritual growth, of knowing and living in God's peace. That is where true wellness is found, absolutely."

Again he paused to allow her time to think.

"But to arrive there—to know and live in God's peace—we must first grasp this issue of who God is and what God honors," he said.

"God does not resist the person who has done wrong. He resists the proud, the person who condemns others while overlooking his own faults.

"Another way to understand this is to realize that if God resists the proud, he honors the humble—the humble in spirit. Being humble in spirit is not being falsely modest; it is being spiritually humble. Those who recognize their need for a God of love and his gift of peace are the spiritually humble.

"If you will allow me, I want to share with you another personal story. It has to do with my own search to understand God in my life. Perhaps it will be of help to you.

"In the depths of my illness, I wanted nothing more than a quick resolution and to get back to a normal life. Then, however, I was presented with the concept that illness is a guidepost, a signal on the road of life. I came to understand that my illness was a message for me to change.

"But I didn't want change. I wanted the comfort and safety of the status quo. My life was a known quantity, never mind that I not so secretly despised many of my circumstances. I just wasn't ready for change or the work change requires.

"Interestingly," the Triumphant Patient continued, "understanding that my illness was a message also provided an answer to the why question. And I was able to see illness as a guidepost calling for my personal spiritual growth. I no longer had to be tormented with the issue of why illness was happening to me. Yet still I resisted. I would not change. I wanted everything to return to normal.

"Then a wise friend said to me, 'You are lazy. It is your laziness coupled with fear that stands in the path of your wellness.'

"That shocked me," he said. "I was a lot of things, but I was not lazy. I wasn't going to be accused of letting laziness stand in the way of my wellness. That was something I could control."

"What did your friend mean when he said you were lazy?" the woman asked.

"He explained that a major form of laziness is fear—fear in the face of uncertainty, fear of the judgment of God, fear of a change in our lives. We want so much to cling to what is known because of the enormity of what might be required of us in new and unfamiliar circumstances. We might venture forth only to lose what we had physically, emotionally, and spiritually. And it would require discipline and work to build a new person."

"I understand," the woman said. "I suppose I share some of that."

"Laziness, masked by fear, holds many of us back from the adventure of living a life full of joy and peace," he said.

"Secretly we fear we may not be able to handle the unknown, or that we may be stretched into new and different people. We wonder how could we possibly give up what we have now? And we end up not venturing forth into new and promising lives.

"This is true of illness. We tend to hold on to disease or disability. It is true on the emotional level as well. We hold on to thoughts based in fear and anger. And certainly it is true on the spiritual level as we find it easier to condemn and judge than to love and forgive.

"It was all true for me," he said. "I tended to resist the possibility that there could be a new and better life for me, one spent living in the presence of God. I found these ideas most threatening because I realized that, if I incorporated them into my life, I would indeed have a great many changes to make. And that sounded like work, lots of work. I was just too lazy, I called it 'fearful,' to explore that path."

The woman nodded in agreement, her attention riveted on the Triumphant Patient.

"I fought against these new possibilities," he said. "I resisted the idea of forgiveness, for that meant I no longer could always be right. I fought unconditional love, for that would mean extending myself in new and vulnerable ways. And I resisted the spiritual. It meant giving up the old willful me and pursuing God's will for my life.

"And all of it required me to abandon my pride. Across all these issues was the need to become a more meek and gentle spirit and to develop a spiritual humility. It would require me to strike the midpoint between self-degradation and grandiosity. I call that 'spiritual self-respect.' We have it when we believe enough in our personal value to know we deserve to live without emotional pain."

He paused and looked directly at her.

"Frankly, I wasn't so sure I was up to all that work," he said.

The woman returned the Triumphant Patient's steady gaze.

"I understand what you're saying, I think," she said. "I can accept that fear or even some laziness may be holding me back, but I think I'm missing a dimension. I don't see how all this fits together. What's the piece that completes this puzzle?"

"There is another piece," he said, gauging his response. Is she ready for a more in-depth look at the spiritual road? he wondered. Could he explain the issues in a manner that wouldn't alienate her?

"My sense is that your ideas of who God is stand in your way of knowing him. Instead of thinking of him as a God who just condemns people, let me tell you about the real God—the God I know.

"Think about this statement. It describes the God I want you to know and experience. *There is a God in our lives who knows us and loves us, a God who loves us even though he knows us.*"

The woman chuckled. The Triumphant Patient could always give a certain twist to words that made them memorable.

"Is that a true statement?" she asked.

"Absolutely," the Triumphant Patient responded. "Let's examine it step by step."

"All right," the woman said.

"The statement begins by affirming that there is a God. Do you believe that?"

"Well, yes. Even though I don't go to church, I believe there is a God. You know, you don't have to go to church to believe in God."

"I certainly agree," he said. "You may want to celebrate God after you come to know him better. Sometimes that is best done in a group setting like a church, but technically you are correct. You don't have to attend formal services to believe there is a God.

"What is more important now is that you said you can affirm there is a God. That is wonderful! It is the starting point.

"The next step is recognizing that this God is in our lives. *In our lives.* When I began to understand the impact of that belief, it was a powerful experience."

"I don't see it," said the woman.

"Just think. This is a God who makes himself a part of my world, a part of my daily life, and yours. He is not a remote being or entity who sits on a throne faraway some where, judging his subjects. He is in our lives, here now, today, to help and comfort, guide and direct. If we will acknowledge and accept this presence, we will never be alone, no matter what the circumstance.

"Can you accept that?" he asked.

"I'm not sure," she answered. "I've not thought I was important enough for God to be concerned with me. He has seemed more like a school principal who gets involved only with significant misbehavior and hands out punishments. But lately I've wondered if I've been at least a little wrong about that.

"You see," she said hesitantly, obviously a little embarrassed, "I've not told this to anyone because I'm not sure what it means or what it is.

"When I began to try to forgive, I made my list and said the words. I meant what I said—or I thought I was sincere, but nothing happened until in desperation I prayed. I had in my mind that I needed to be forgiven and to forgive myself and then the rest would come. When I asked God to forgive me—little insignificant me—I felt forgiven and I felt loved.

"It seemed all right after that to pray again and again. When I do, I feel a presence. It's more than a peaceful serenity. It's like someone is there with me.

"Is that God?"

The Triumphant Patient was amazed. He had known all along the woman had great potential for understanding the concepts of the triumphant journey to wellness. Still he had thought he would have to work hard making the points he wanted to share with her this day, and to introduce her to a God who could be active in her life. But she had discovered him on her own or he had made himself known to her. However it happened, it was joyous.

"Yes, that is God. He is in your life right now. Actually he has been all along, but you've not been responsive to him and you didn't know.

"Do you feel now that he knows you?"

"I'm beginning to," she answered.

"Then you must feel as excited about him knowing you and loving you personally as I do about him knowing me and loving me. Isn't it fantastic?

"He is not an impersonal God. We are known to him by name, in thought and spirit, in all the ways God identifies and recognizes his children. This is not some remote power. We are talking about a personal

one-to-one relationship with the Central Power behind everything that exists."

"Sometimes I don't want him to know me," the
woman said. "I don't want him to know the unattractive parts of me."

"Then you need to think about the next part of the
statement: There is a God in our lives who knows us
and *loves us.*

"How can it be? The God of All is, first of all, in our
lives, then he knows us by name, and now we learn
this same God actually loves us! Wonder of wonders!
How could we have such great fortune? Why this is
the greatest treasure that ever existed."

The woman smiled at the Triumphant Patient's un-
abashed enthusiasm. But then this was something to
be excited about. She could feel her excitement building too. She was hearing about a different God, one
who could know her and love her.

"The concluding part of the statement is, however,
the most exciting part. It says, 'God loves us *even
though* he knows us.'

"We have the assurance of God's love even though
we do all those 'unattractive' things in our lives. But,
even though we do all those silly things, even when
our behavior doesn't match our potentials, we are still
loved.

"Do you see that this relates directly to your belief
about having had more than your share of God's con-
demnation? You see, God has not condemned you
with an affliction. He is not punishing you. Your illness is simply a fact of life, not an act of God.

"But God can use your illness in powerful ways,

such as giving you a new spiritual strength, and making you a channel of his love."

Yes. The woman clearly remembered this from her talk with Britta.

"I came to realize that God is *for* us!" he continued. "God wants our total wellness—in body, mind, and spirit. Now that may be something short of a cure or a total recovery, but God wants to use our life circumstances in the best way possible. Therefore, my sole focus became an endeavor to understand and follow God's will. This says nothing about cures; it says nothing about total physical recoveries. But it says everything about spiritual and emotional well-being. And it says everything about the quality of our lives no matter what the quantity."

The Triumphant Patient paused and fixed his gaze on the woman. Finally she spoke.

"What does this really mean to me?" she asked.

"It means you have an important choice to make. One alternative will be to attempt a return to life as normal, the way it was prior to your illness. The other path, the triumphant path, leads you from extending forgiveness and unconditional love to accepting them."

"Accepting unconditional love and forgiveness?" she said. "What do you mean, 'accepting' them?"

"Accepting them from God," replied the Triumphant Patient. "Know that just as you extend love and forgiveness to others, God extends love and forgiveness in even greater measure to you.

"Even though our behaviors may not match our potentials, even though our capacity for kindness and goodness is not fully realized, we can still receive

God's life-changing love. And we are able to do this because God loves us for who we are, not for what we do.

"Because of God's great love, we are still acceptable, even though we may be imperfect.

"We are imperfect but acceptable," he repeated.

"Imperfect but acceptable?" she asked.

He nodded yes.

Tears came to the woman's eyes. She breathed deeply and sighed, releasing all her tension. Quietly, almost inaudibly, she spoke.

"A God who knows me and loves me, even when I am imperfect. I want to believe that so very much."

"Believe it," he said, "for what you have before you this moment is truth."

"I have never felt love like this before. It has always seemed that strings were attached to the love of family and friends."

"There are no strings here," he said. "Learn to recognize this great love. Let God's love fill your life to overflowing. And once your cup is filled, then serve others with that same unconditional love and forgiveness."

"Yes, I understand," said the woman.

"And this love can heal," he said. "It will surely bring you a knowledge of God's peace. This is God's gift. This love ultimately conquers illness.

"Right this moment you have the ability to be transformed. You see, this love brings us to the edge of mystery. And the mystery is this: We cannot will ourselves to this wellness, but we can open ourselves to its presence. We don't earn it. We accept it."

Listening with newfound eagerness, the woman

was quenching a thirst that had long been with her.

"Learn to nurture a home for this great love," he said. "But nurture that home without a primary concern of finding a reward, such as a cure. Instead nurture God's love because it is truth. The reward will find you."

While they sat for a moment in silence, the Triumphant Patient prayed silently for wisdom.

"I want to believe this so much," said the woman. "But in many ways trust is so difficult. From my earliest recollections, I have seen God as out to get me, never for me. And now to trust. That is asking a great deal."

"God is faithful, even through these times of illness," he said. "He is worthy of your trust. You will never be hurt if you trust too much. But you will live in torment if you trust too little.

"Trust, my friend, that whatever the outcome, it will be acceptable. The lesson is trust. Trusting in God's love is the most important issue.

"This love and trust brings to you a new life. Your understanding has now evolved. For now, filled with God's unconditional love, you can live free of fear and free of limits. In a very real sense, illness will never again touch the real you."

The woman was visibly moved.

"How can this happen to me?" she asked. "How can I make this real in my life?"

The Triumphant Patient spoke gently.

"Welcome this great Love into your heart. Acknowledge God and commit to follow Love's path.

"When I was at this point in my journey, I made a promise. I called it a 'Covenant for Wellness,' and to this day I follow it. It is my new way of living. And it is very simple.

"First, I asked God to do two things for me:

1. Eliminate illness on any level he felt I needed—body, mind, and spirit.
2. Make real in my life his highest potential for my wellness in body, mind, and spirit.

"Then I wrote out what I would do for God.

1. Choose hope over despair in all areas of my life.
2. Practice sincere gratitude for all the blessings I now have.
3. Spend an hour each day in prayer, meditation, and study, preparing my mind and spirit to receive God's direction.
4. Practice forgiveness in all my relationships.
5. Be a channel for God's unconditional love.
6. Pursue God's will for my life as I understand it.
7. Commit to sharing this message with others.

"I try to live my life by this covenant, concentrating on fulfilling my part of the agreement. It has absolutely changed my life for the better. In fact, I believe it is the reason I am alive today."

The woman sat quietly, considering all she had heard.

"Grow in God's love," he said. "Such growth usually is done in the dark, especially the darkness of the struggle. That is what your illness is—the darkness. But if you are willing to do the work, if you can even learn to give thanks for the darkness that accompanies growth and to accept it, new dimensions of your true self will gather and build.

"And finally, out of the darkness comes the Light. It comes when you are ready to see it, to acknowledge it.

"Do the work. Be willing to change. And remember, you were a divine idea before you were human and to that you must return. Walk in the Light."

They sat together in silence. There was peace about them; God's wonderful peace was with them. And all was well.

"Go now," he said. "Continue the journey you have started.

"I pray God's every blessing to you."

Covenant for Wellness

I ask God to—

1. Eliminate illness on any level he feels I need—body, mind, and spirit.
2. Make real in my life his highest potential for my wellness in body, mind, and spirit.

I will—

1. Choose hope over despair in all areas of my life.
2. Practice sincere gratitude for all the blessings I now have.
3. Spend an hour each day in prayer, meditation, and study, preparing my mind and spirit to receive God's direction.
4. Practice forgiveness in all my relationships.
5. Be a channel for God's unconditional love.
6. Pursue God's will for my life as I understand it.
7. Commit to sharing this message with others.

Signed _____ Date _____

Chapter 8

Triumphant Celebration

The woman made a commitment. She signed her covenant and dedicated herself to walking the spiritual path. She shared with her family all she had learned and asked their cooperation in putting into practice these life-changing principles.

The woman not only learned, she did. She dedicated herself to practicing and implementing this new way of living. The rewards became more apparent each and every day. And before long she knew she had triumphed. She too was a triumphant patient!

What a new and exciting life it was! Every day was a wonderful gift from God, for which she was deeply grateful. God's peace became more and more real for her and she experienced a wonder and reverence for life, a new level of awareness, far beyond her expectations. With each new day she was filled with joy for the gift of another day of life.

She reflected on the first year of her journey and remembered the day she first met the Triumphant Patient. So much had changed for her. Then she was gripped by fear. Now she felt a growing sense of mastery and was buoyed by a serene confidence. She consistently chose hope, even when tempted by those who could only think of defeat and despair. Her beliefs about illness were entirely new and always emphasized the positive.

Forgiveness had become such an effective way to resolve her emotional conflicts that her family even began to follow her example. And unconditional love was a most rewarding experience. She could hardly believe the difference this made in her outlook and her relationships. But her decision to follow God's will, to accept God's love, even though she was imperfect, was truly the crowning glory.

She had new life. And she was so grateful. This was living—life triumphant.

The woman began working with other triumphant patients, helping those people who had been newly diagnosed. It was thrilling to see people change their lives, making a triumph of what most people would consider to be their worst tragedies. And she devoted more of her time to this work. She wanted to give back in whatever way was possible.

She found great satisfaction in helping others to help themselves. She did not think of it in terms of rescuing, but that in the truest sense it was the sharing of a gift from her heart with no strings attached. For the first time she felt her life was benefiting the world in which she lived. She was so fortunate that she had learned so much.

One afternoon her phone rang. A young woman was on the line. She had just received a diagnosis of a life-threatening illness.

"I am about to start a journey toward wellness and I know there is much to learn," the caller said. "I understand you have become triumphant and I would like to learn from you. May I come and talk to you?"

It was a touching moment for the woman. She felt an overwhelming sense of gratitude and humility that God was using her life to help others. She whispered a silent prayer for the young caller. Yes, she said, she would help in any way appropriate. She would do all possible to help the young woman find wellness.

When her guest arrived, she said, "I'm happy to share this life-changing message with you. In doing so, I have one request."

"What is that?" asked the young woman.

"That you share this hope with others."

And that is the message to you too.

*Share
this hope with
others.*

AFTERWORD

The first time I heard "imperfect but acceptable," I did not understand the meaning. I've learned a great deal since then and today it is the basis for my wellness—spiritually, emotionally, and physically.

It is my experience that Jesus Christ is the One after whom I should model wellness. The result is that He has used my life more powerfully than I could have dreamed.

Might this also be true for you? Could illness, disability, or other problems be a message to you to walk a more spiritual journey, practicing forgiveness and unconditional love? Could your "liability" possibly be turned into an "asset" that changes your life?

I encourage you to travel this path. It is truly triumphant, leading to wellness on the highest level.

Blessings in your journey.

ABOUT THE AUTHOR

Greg Anderson is a triumphant patient. Diagnosed with metastasized lung cancer in 1984, he was given only thirty days to live. Refusing to accept the hopelessness of this diagnosis, he went in search of people who had lived when they were "supposed" to die. His findings, from interviews with hundreds of survivors, form the principles of this life-changing book.

In 1985, Greg started the Cancer Conquerors Foundation, an organization that provides training and support for implementing body/mind/spirit principles. Services include seminars, workshops, audio/visual programs, self-assessment tools, and ongoing personal consultation.

The Anderson family lives in the Los Angeles area. Greg and his wife, Linda, are parents of one daughter, Erica. Prior to his illness, Greg was Vice President and Executive Director of the Robert Schuller Institute located at the Crystal Cathedral in Garden Grove, California. He is also the author of the inspirational best seller *The Cancer Conqueror*. Today he travels extensively to speak and conduct workshops sharing his experience and techniques.

The Triumphant Patient Project is an extension of these principles to all people with life-threatening illness or life-changing disability. A series of Triumphant Patient events will be held in major cities throughout North America.

For more information and a free newsletter, "Creating Wellness," please write:

> The Triumphant Patient Project
> P.O. Box 3444
> Fullerton, CA 92634